The Virtual Lawyer

DOUGLAS MCPHERSON

Commissioning editor
Alex Davies

Published by
Globe Law and Business Ltd
3 Mylor Close
Horsell
Woking
Surrey GU21 4DD
United Kingdom
Tel: +44 20 3745 4770
www.globelawandbusiness.com

ISBN: 978-1-78358-402-4
A catalogue record for this book is available from the British Library

Contents

Executive summary

It is of course an understatement to say our lives have changed massively since the end of March 2020. The restrictions that have had to be brought in to control COVID-19 saw almost all of us forced to work from home, only connected to our colleagues and clients by Teams, Zoom, and Facetime.

At the time it looked like this was going to be a six-month blip. We'd ride it out then things would start to go back to normal and we could carry on as we were.

We all now know that is definitely not the case. As I started writing this book in late October 2020 we had started to see a slight return to the office – albeit in shifts to maintain the required social distancing – and face-to-face meetings over coffee or lunch were starting to creep back in. However, it now looks as though in the short-term at least the restrictions will get tighter before they relax again.

But you know all this. What does it have to do with business development?

Way back in March, a lot of law firms pushed business development to the bottom of their priorities. Work had to come first. And, as we can't do business development the way we always have, there was no way to keep it going even if we wanted to.

The only problem is, if you don't do any business development, you are not going to generate the new work required to sustain your practice. You are also going to put yourself at high risk of losing the client relationships you have worked so hard to build. This meant we had to quickly come up with new ways to do business development from home. We had to adapt our approach by using the tools that were available to us. We had to replace physical business development with virtual business development.

The Virtual Lawyer examines those new virtual ways of approaching marketing and business development, explaining how you can continue to strengthen your existing relationships, boost your visibility in the markets you serve, and generate the new introductions and new opportunities you'll need to grow your practice whilst working remotely.

The book uses a three-step model, designed to take us from where we are today to where we need to be in the future, whatever that future ends up looking like. These three steps are React, Refresh, and Return.

React

What do lawyers need to do to react to the new restrictions, new working environment, and new client demands? How can you adapt your personal BD plan to circumvent the current restrictions? Most importantly, it looks at the practical ways to network and build your profile virtually by using what you have available – your laptop, tablet, and smartphone. This stage will be supplemented with tips on how to create and maintain an ongoing 30-day personal BD plan.

Refresh

Once your virtual business development is up and running, how do you make sure your plan is capable of making the best of the current situation? How can you become more flexible in your approach by starting to reintroduce more traditional BD activities while continuing to take full advantage of the new virtual activities you introduced while working remotely?

This stage is supported by tips on how to create and maintain an ongoing 90-day personal BD plan.

Return

Eventually things will go back to something close to normal. At that point you need to be completely "BD-ready" so you stay close to your clients and contacts and, just as importantly, one step ahead of your competitors. We will look at what you need to do to prepare for the future. What will our personal BD plans look like? This stage looks at how we balance the demands of client development, leveraging our professional networks, and winning new clients and/or breaking into new markets by creating an approach that will work in what is likely to be a hybrid of office and home working.

However the current pandemic plays out, your commercial future will rely on your ability to keep generating new work as a lawyer, as a department, and as a firm. These three steps have been designed to help you do that virtually.

You will learn the skills you'll need to continue to build your practice even during times when meetings, events, and hospitality aren't possible. You'll be able to utilize the technology you have to hand to stay as accessible and responsive as you always have been, while you identify and progress new opportunities from your desk.

Regardless of how or where you have to work at any given time, you will be ready to operate as a Virtual Lawyer.

About the author

Douglas McPherson has had a long career in marketing and business development within professional services. For the last ten years he has been a director of Size 10½ Boots Ltd, a specialist BD agency that works solely with law firms, accountants, intellectual property firms, and barristers' chambers, helping them find smarter, easier, and more effective ways to grow their practice. This book brings a lot of his most recent experience together, most specifically in terms of finding ways for clients to adapt their marketing and BD so they can continue to grow despite the current restrictions and a tough and uncertain trading environment.

Part 1:
React

Chapter 1: How to keep doing effective business development while we can't meet in person

Why do you need to adapt your personal business development plan?

Traditionally for law firms business development has centered on four main activities – networking, meetings, hospitality, and seminars.

Networking

Networking means different things to different people. It can be formal networking events either locally (e.g. the local business club or organized professionals' group), or (inter)nationally. If you are taking a more focused sector-based approach, it could be add-ons to conferences or groups organized by the relevant trade bodies.

Or, if formal events aren't your thing, networking could mean more informal get-togethers, bringing a few contacts and clients together over lunch or drinks.

Meetings

The types of meetings you have with your clients and contacts will vary depending on the preferences of the individual you're meeting. Some may be over coffee, lunch, or breakfast. Some may be in your offices or others at their premises.

Hospitality

Client entertaining has long been a staple of legal marketing. Again, the approach should always be tailored to the preferences of your guests. It could involve trips to sporting events, meals, wine tasting, a summer or Christmas reception, cocktail making or your annual golf day.

More and more, firms are trying to find something a little different to do so that their event is the one that their invitees go to even if it's just out of curiosity. Some of the activities we've seen recently include darts, pétanque, cookery courses, and even axe throwing.

Seminars

The last option is seminars (an activity that thankfully now employs a bit more creativity and variety thanks to the introduction of round tables, panel discussions, Q&As and client training). When there is a legal update to share or a particular issue to analyze, the firm will invite all of its clients, contacts, and targets into their offices to go through that topic in detail.

The only problem is these are all "physical" activities that involve meeting in person and, depending on where you are and what the current guidelines are, that is probably not an option at the moment.

It may be tempting to think that means doing business development is now too hard so it may be best just to pause your efforts temporarily. However, your practice simply won't survive if you are not investing in your client and professional relationships. This is where the vast majority of your new matters will come from and new matters are still the lifeblood of every legal practice.

This means that while we are restricted in what we can do BD-wise, we need to find alternative ways to keep all four activities moving.

What are the alternatives?

In very general terms, there are three things you can do to overcome the challenge of not being able to meet in person.

Do more on the telephone

While phone calls are the obvious thing to do with a phone, you can actually do a lot more. Video calls have, over the last few months, become a major part of every working day and are now arguably the most popular way to keep in touch.

You can also message people – both inside and outside the firm. Make sure you know the preferences of the people you're messaging as you don't want to overstep the mark, but I have found more and more clients want to keep in touch by WhatsApp or text messages. It's a really easy way to get quick answers or keep conversations ticking over in the background.

If you are more adventurous, you can also record video and audio on your phone. I've seen an increasing number of lawyers producing regular video updates and promoting them via the firm's blog or LinkedIn. Similarly, a growing number of firms are now producing podcasts, many of which have been recorded either as voice memos or via Zoom using a phone.

Give the same advice in writing

The volume of blogs and articles written by lawyers exploded over lockdown. People recognized their clients (and therefore their prospective clients) needed advice and reassurances in equal measure and blogging provided the perfect vehicle. It's free, it's immediate and (handled properly) it's fully search engine optimizable, which means your potential audience is limitless.

However, with a little more time to spare for business development, many lawyers also took the opportunity to look outside the firm to find new audiences.

They identified the publications and websites their clients read (primarily niche trade publications for commercially focused lawyers or local papers and magazines for those involved in the three private client disciplines) and offered their editors editorial ideas.

Do more online

For me, online opportunities roughly split into two. The first is events, which can include virtual networking events – either traditional networking events organized by independent groups or smaller, more informal groups that you have organized – and webinars. These can be live or pre-recorded workshops or can be panel events or roundtable-style discussions. I have also seen some good one-on-one conversations that dig into a specific topic in much more detail.

As well as giving you an opportunity to get in touch with your marketing database during the invitation phase and bringing everyone together for the event, what you record will also feed the other parts of your business development plan. You will have video clips to add to your website, promote via social media and your YouTube channel and you can recycle your notes to make new blogs or give you something to tempt the editors of relevant publications and websites with.

The second is social media and in particular, LinkedIn. Your social media channels allow you to promote your new blogs, new videos, virtual events, and external articles to your followers, but it can also give you much more in terms of targeting and initiating new conversations with those targets.

By definition, there is a social aspect to social media. Some of the most successful tactics I've seen on LinkedIn have been much more focused on the personal side rather than on business. Sometimes the most potent business development comes from finding a likeminded group and using that common ground to engage your audience.

So now that we've established that the three currently-available BD options are the phone, content, and online, how can you use those to replace networking, meetings, hospitality, and seminars? The table below provides a short summary of how to replace "face time" with virtual initiatives, but to give you a better idea of how you can start to adapt your plan I will also share some practical examples and suggestions to support each point.

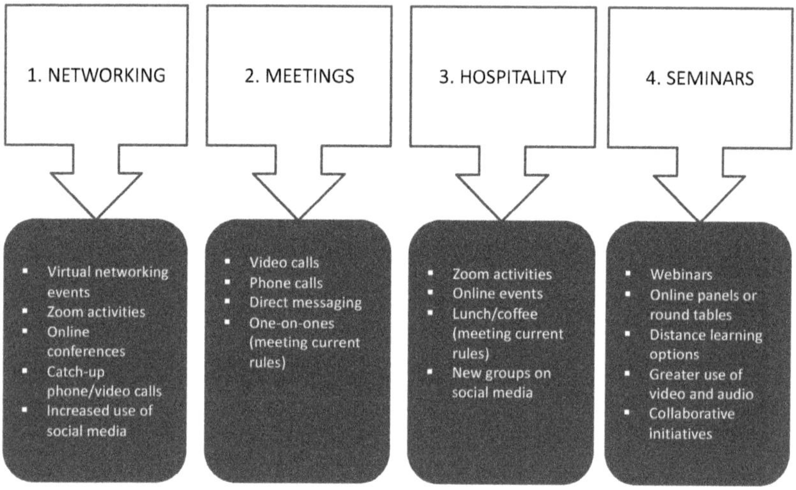

Figure 1: Alternative activities.

Replacing traditional networking

Technology can play a huge part in terms of helping you continue to develop your personal professional network. Even though we can't go to or host events in the way we used to, we can replace those events with a combination of the following.

Virtual networking events

The virtual networking events that sprung up at the beginning of lockdown were a bit clunky and beset with buffering, time delays, and often two or three overbearing personalities monopolizing the conversation. However, newer platforms like Remo have really enhanced the quality of online networking. These platforms allow you to move tables and join in new conversations, invite people into "side rooms" to continue new conversations on a one-on-one basis and swap virtual business cards so you can do the follow up in (almost) the same way you would after a physical event.

Alternatively, you could organize your own events by listing out a few clients and contacts with a common interest. One example I have seen work particularly well is an Anglo-French business group made up of a number of bilingual professionals from a range of disciplines. They used to meet in Central London on a monthly basis but now meet online. They have a set formula – to give each other a quick update on what they've been up to and bring any new opportunities to the table – which keeps the meetings short and productive.

It is this type of more informal networking that works well on Zoom. As everyone knows each other the potential for talking over each other is reduced, as is any awkwardness around virtual small talk.

Zoom activities

In a bid to overcome that "just another Zoom call" feeling, some firms have started to anchor their Zoom meetings around an activity. Just as it would in real life, this makes the event a little different and also gives participants something to talk about, which makes the most important part of networking – establishing a personal connection – that little bit easier.

One of my favorite examples of a Zoom activity is a matrimonial law firm that arranged a Zoom cookery course over the summer. They invited the people they wanted to take part, gave them a list of ingredients a week before the class, then had a chef talk the group through the recipe over Zoom.

Another example was the formation of an international wine connoisseurs group by two patent attorneys. They regularly work with other attorneys across the US, Australia, Europe and South Africa so they all take turns to suggest a few different bottles of wine then taste and compare notes together over Zoom.

Online conferences

This is one of the BD opportunities that has been hit hardest, particularly when the conference has an international attendance. However, platforms like Remo have come to the fore. Not only do they allow you to network more effectively (often allowing you to book slots with the attendees you really want to meet in advance of the conference), they also allow the keynote speakers to pre-market their sessions more effectively and provide an opportunity for the audience to ask questions before, during, and after the sessions. All of this makes it much easier for the speakers and attendees to build up a long-term rapport.

Catch up phone/video calls

As with all networking activities, success comes from the follow-up, not from turning up. You need to be prepared to arrange follow-up meetings with the people you meet at events and, as we can't do this over coffee/lunch/drinks at the moment, this needs to be done with a phone or a video call.

If you are networking regularly you will be meeting quite a few new people. To keep your follow-up manageable, I'd suggest you always ask yourself two questions when you start to plan your follow-up:

1. Could they be a useful addition to my professional network? This doesn't just mean they could become a client, it could mean that they are well networked, well connected and capable of providing new invitations or introductions further down the line)
2. Did I like them? After all, who wants to put themselves through the torture test of a phone or video call with someone you didn't get on with!

If you answer yes to both, those names need to go on your shortlist. The rest you can connect with on LinkedIn and pass their details on to your marketing team so they can (compliant with GDPR) add them to your database so you firm stays in touch with them for you.

Once you have your shortlist you can send each a personalized LinkedIn request letting them know you will be in touch with an invitation to carry on your conversation. The template we use is:

> *"It was good to meet you at the recent Local Business Group event. I will be in touch to arrange a call as I'm very interested to find out more about your new product range, but in the meantime, I'd like to invite you to join my LinkedIn network."*

Now you have left your foot in the door to follow up with that all important invite. Here is our template for you to edit:

> *"I really enjoyed meeting you at the recent Local Business Group event on [date]. It's always tricky to have a proper conversation at these things – especially now we're online – but as I said in my LinkedIn invite, I'm very interested to find out more about your new product range.*
>
> *"As we can't meet up at the moment I'd like to arrange a quick phone or video call. I was thinking about either [offer two dates with times].*

If you could let me know which works best (or suggest an alternative if neither are convenient) and whether you'd prefer a phone or video call, I'll send an invite. I look forward to your reply."

I can appreciate at first sight that offering two specific times and dates may look a little strong, but it does work. The psychology suggests giving people a choice between two actual slots makes it more likely they will choose one, whereas leaving it open-ended tends to increase the likelihood of your invitation going unanswered.

Before you make the call, try and think what you want to get out of it. Set yourself a couple of objectives so that you leave each call with an agreed follow-up step so you can keep your conversation moving forward. The other benefit of setting clear objectives is it also gives you something to work towards, so if the call goes off track, you can easily bring it back to where you want it to be.

Increased use of social media

As mentioned earlier, LinkedIn provides you with the perfect opportunity to take full advantage of shared personal interests by creating new groups. These usually start with your current contacts but, once they're up and running, they can be found by new contacts who can then ask to join, bringing their opportunities with them.

Two examples we have seen work well over the last few months are:

1. The Spotify playlists produced each week by my business partner, Bernard Savage. These now have a large following within the professional services and, by following up on specific comments people have made on certain tracks, we've been able to start some productive new conversations.
2. A business group for the supporters of English soccer club Chelsea, set up by a fan with a strong social media following. The group has brought together supporters from every industry and every profession and grew to almost 500 members in its first week, all of whom immediately started to connect and exchange messages with the other members because they all had something in common.

I am fully expecting accusations of self-interest here, given the examples I've used are close to my heart. But then again, as I have said before, the best business development often uses our personal interests for commercial gain!

However, if using this more personal approach on LinkedIn doesn't sit well with you, you can of course use LinkedIn in a more systematic way to broker new "cold" connections.

You can identify people you'd like to connect with either within your connections' networks, within the memberships of the groups you participate in, or because they have been liked or shared by your connections. You can then invite them to connect with a personalized note explaining why you'd like to connect.

One note of caution at this point. The number of connection requests we've all received over the last few months may have increased massively, but unfortunately so has the number of people who immediately follow up with clumsy cut-and-paste sales messages, thanking you for connecting and offering you all sorts of unmissable offers. I know I am not alone – or even in the minority – when I say that this type of approach is always met by me removing their connection.

Instead, I would suggest you bide your time. Like and share a few of their posts so that you become more visible to them and, when the time is right, send them a direct message to invite them to an upcoming webinar or to alert them to a relevant piece of content.

Alternatively, you could pick up on one of their posts and ask if you could catch up on the phone to "discuss that in more detail as it caught my attention".

Replacing client meetings

Video calls

Video calls are probably the closest thing we now have to a meeting with clients and contacts. They allow you to speak face-to-face and you can also share your screen when you need to go through documents together. I rarely used video technology for meetings before we were forced to work from home. However, with practice comes confidence and the majority of my working days are now spent on Zoom, Teams, and Facetime.

I won't pretend I find it as easy as meeting face-to-face, but it has definitely become increasingly normal as the months have gone on.

Phone calls

I won't insult anyone by explaining what a phone call is! I will, however, put a strong business case forward for them. Over the last few months phones have played a really important part in helping us maintain our most important working relationships. When it comes from making more of your phone, I have two pieces of advice:

1. Whenever there is a credible reason to replace an email with a call, do it. Not only will it help you sort what you need to sort more quickly and more effectively, it also gives you a chance to catch up and find out if there's anything else you could be helping with.
2. Don't shy away from small talk while you're on the phone. It is not an exaggeration to say that while we have been working from home I have had longer, broader, and deeper conversations with our clients, and that includes the most senior partners within the firms I work with.

As our social circle has reduced, people have more time and inclination to chat. Why not take advantage of this to strengthen your working relationships? If you can identify areas of personal common interest, that really will improve the effectiveness of your business development.

One-on-ones (meeting current rules)

Just before restrictions in the UK were increased again over the fall, one-on-one meetings were starting to creep back in. As people were starting to return to the office for one or two days a week and coffee shops and restaurants began to resume a more normal service, one could see the usual business meetings starting to happen at a few of the tables.

However, as welcome as it is to be able to meet up and have real conversations with our clients and professional contacts again, a strong degree of emotional intelligence has to be applied.

Firstly, if your local guidelines don't permit meeting in person, it can't be an option. If meetings of very small groups are allowed locally, you have to take every possible invite on a case-by-case basis. My suggestion is that if you need/want to meet someone in person, include a line in your email that reads something like:

> *"I'd prefer to meet up for coffee or lunch but completely understand if you are not comfortable with that. If you could let me know whether you'd prefer to meet in person or on video I can send across some potential times and dates."*

Replacing hospitality

Zoom activities

We have already looked in-depth at the networking opportunities Zoom offers. It is the same when it comes to replacing your traditional hospitality events. All you need to do is:

1. Choose an activity.
2. Invite those you want to attend.
3. Host your event.

You will have a reason to bring people together and – this is a hugely important element – have some fun while you do so.

With regards to the follow-up from these events, one idea I have seen work well is to take some screen shots of people during the events (cookery is a great example as you can catch your guests at a particularly messy stage) and share these photos with your guests or, with their express permission, via social media.

The direct benefit of being able to share these shots with a wider audience is you will usually get a few more people from your network stepping forward to ask if they can be invited to the next event. This of course keeps increasing your reach and moving your business development forward into new areas.

Online events

When replacing traditional hospitality events, the online options are either going to involve Zoom or, for more formal or educational initiatives, the examples we'll look at in the next section on replacing seminars. But there are two examples that perhaps fall between these stools that I wanted to share.

The first involves a firm that is well-known within its region for running an annual golf day. These events bring together a huge number of its clients and referrers and, by mixing them up into different four-balls, it offers the guests a very easy way to meet new people and extend their networks. This year, they ran the event via an online gaming platform (for those willing to play that way). The draws were made as usual and then the prize-giving was held via Zoom while the players enjoyed the contents of the pre-prepared hampers that had been sent to their homes ahead of the evening.

The second involves a prominent commercial property lawyer who regularly meets his key clients and referrers for an online game of poker. Again, this was organized via Zoom, and proved to be such a success that, at the height of lockdown, it became a weekly fixture and a proven generator of new work thanks to the conversations taking place between hands.

Lunch/coffee (meeting current rules)

We are – in my opinion at least – still a very long way from the receptions and other large scale hospitality events we enjoyed in the past. However, as discussed in the last section, restrictions are beginning to permit smaller, more personal, meetings, so as before my advice would be to respect the current situation and always give your invitee the choice.

New groups on social media

Some of our clients have chosen to move their existing self-run networking groups onto social media. The obvious choice is to create a group on LinkedIn to provide your members with a way to stay in touch and an easily accessible hub they can use to ask for help, exchange ideas, and share updates.

Some have been a little bolder and – returning to a previous theme – looked to exploit shared personal interests. They have created hashtags on Twitter that their followers can use to join them while they watch a sports game, listen to a pre-arranged music album, or watch a pre-arranged film.

Similarly, I've also heard of clients using Instagram to swap photos of their culinary endeavors.

Replacing seminars

Webinars

If we didn't know how effective webinars were before the current situation, we certainly do now. As webinars were already a staple of legal marketing, the switch from seminars to webinars was probably the easiest and most obvious physical–virtual switch.

Although we all know what webinars are and how they work, there are a few useful lessons we've learned over the last few months:

1. **Don't forget a clear call-to-action**. As there isn't the opportunity to spend time with your guests on the day of your presentation, you need to make sure your conversation with the audience continues after your presentation. One easy way to do this is to merge your slides with your notes to create a more detailed white paper and offer that (with an email address) at the end of the webinar. Or you could offer a free consultancy session or the opportunity to ask questions offline and in confidence. The important thing is to center your call-to-action on something that will benefit the audience and make it crystal clear what they need to do to access those benefits.

2. **Use a recognized webinar platform**. The last thing you want on the day is buffering or difficulties accessing your session, so we would always advocate using a dedicated online platform. Our choice is GoToWebinar. It not only hosts your content and your guests as you present, but also allows you to automate the invitation process and even create a branded virtual waiting room for your guests, which gives your event that additional level of professionalism. And the costs are relatively low.
3. **Record it**. When you use a dedicated platform you will also have the choice of recording your presentation. Accept that offer! It means you have something you can send those who couldn't make it on the day and something you can send to those you wanted to attend but didn't. You can also add the file to your website so that people can either watch it when it suits them or pass on the link to their colleagues, clients, and contacts, which will of course help you reach a brand new audience (and Google loves video, which impacts on your search engine rankings). You can also take clips out of the full presentation to promote the full version on your YouTube channel or on social media.

Online panels or round tables

As turning seminars into webinars was the most obvious choice, it will come as no surprise that the number of webinars sky-rocketed during the first few months of the pandemic. This caused a great deal of "Zoom fatigue" and attendances predictably dropped as people tired of being talked at through their screens.

The cannier law firms countered this by adapting the format of their online presentations. Instead of doing all the talking, they brought in a panel of experts so they could rebrand their sessions as panel discussions or round tables. From my experience, these formats have been better received and better attended.

This format tends to encourage more interaction and engagement. People can ask questions in real time, rather than having to wait until the end. Participants also feel empowered to add their own perspectives to your discussions and, because your session will be based on several experts providing their opinions in short bursts, it is actually easier to listen to.

From a practical point of view, they are also easier to prepare for. As you are only providing your part of the answer to the questions raised, there is no longer a need to prepare a slide deck or a hand-out for afterwards. If you do want to produce something for circulating after the event, why not second an enthusiastic trainee to take notes and turn those into a branded PDF summary of your discussions?

If you are interested in adapting your online approach to include round tables and panel events, here are a few things we've learned over the last few months:

1. **Choose the right panelists**. Panelists make this type of event and should not just be chosen solely on their technical specialisms (although that is of course a very necessary criterion). Make sure they also have:
   - The right personality, are comfortable in front of an audience, and willing to get involved in a discussion;
   - An opinion. You want to provide your audience with valuable insight, not just the usual party line; and
   - A following. After all, you want to maximize your audience.
2. **Rehearse**. It is always a good idea to rehearse any type of presentation, but with a panel-based event it is even more important. Make sure people aren't exceeding their given timeslots and ensure the handover between speakers is smooth. Practice passing the mic (figuratively) by getting in the habit of mentioning people's names and asking them what they think about a particular point.
3. **Encourage participation**. At the start of the event, tell your audience you welcome their participation and encourage people to ask questions and put their hands up to volunteer their thoughts and perspectives. Then repeat that halfway through so the questions keep coming during the second half of the session. You should also remind people there will be a Q&A at the end in case some of your attendees prefer to ask their questions that way.
4. **Have a valuable follow-up document**. While your audience will appreciate a summary of your discussions so they can refer back to the key points, having an accurate summary of what was covered will also provide you with collateral you can use to a) let the people who couldn't attend know what they've missed (so they sign up for the next event) and b) use to market your next event to the people you would like to come.
5. **Have a clear call-to-action**. These events are primarily run to start conversations, so always offer something of value and make very clear what your audience needs to do to claim it.

Distance learning options

An alternative way of presenting the materials you may have used in your seminars in the recent past is to produce a distance learning course. This could be made up of a number of different options:

- Pre-recorded full-length seminar-style talks;
- Pre-recorded short, informal "talking head" videos;
- PDF downloads taken from the supporting notes you would have ordinarily prepared as your script;
- Flowcharts outlining the key processes involved in the ideas you are promoting; and/or
- PDF case studies and worksheets.

If pressed, I would always suggest you employ a mixture of all of these so you produce a range of materials that meets the personal learning preferences of everyone who accesses your course.

Once you have your materials, the easiest thing to do is to save them in an accessible part of your website (preferably behind a password-protected wall to underline the value and exclusivity of the materials). You can then either offer them to your existing clients as an added value extra or sell access on a per user license as a way to generate additional income while you prove your worth and capability to a brand new audience.

Greater use of video and audio

The more standard educational formats are not the only options to consider. You can cover the same material in a more conversational style in podcasts and short one-on-one video discussions.

Over the last few months, the number of firms experimenting with audio and video has increased significantly. Thanks to our phones and the availability of the required apps, both options are almost free to produce and allow you to cover, store, and promote content for your audience to digest at a time convenient to them.

There are also additional benefits when it comes to using video and audio in terms of growing your reach. Both are accessed through sites that anyone can use (for podcasts it could be Apple, Spotify, or Soundcloud, or for video it will probably be YouTube). This means that anyone searching for related content will find you, so as long as your message holds their interest and presses the right buttons, it should create new enquiries.

Collaborative initiatives

In Europe there is an enormous groundswell of enthusiasm for organizing more collaborative initiatives, either with key referrers or with the professional bodies associated with your key markets. These can range from co-hosted webinars, round tables or panel events to co-written articles or newsletters. Some of our clients are also looking into producing white papers and special reports with firms of accountants, wealth managers, real estate agents, and/or trade bodies to produce longer thought-leadership pieces.

From a client perspective these collaborations will give your clients and contacts a broader perspective of the issues they face and introduce the multi-faceted potential solutions they need to address those issues, which will reflect well on you. It positions you as a participant operating in their industry rather than just another adviser looking in from outside.

From a practical perspective, it is easier for you to execute collaborative BD because there are more pairs of hands to deliver the finished marketing material. From a commercial perspective, your audience will immediately double or treble depending on how many partners you bring in, and because you will have been introduced by someone the recipient knows and trusts, you will be regarded as a credible participant because of your association with your partner.

What if I'm not comfortable with technology?

As someone who isn't highly technical, I completely understand if this is your next question. At the start of this book I promised you can do everything I'll discuss with your phone, your tablet, or your PC, and I stand by that promise. If you have an experienced marketing resource or the budget to cover professional filming or audio production, that will take care of the majority of your needs. However, if you don't have access to these types of resources, Figure 2 overleaf will show what you can use from your home office.

Best of all, the majority of these apps and programs are free. Where there is a cost, for example with Remo or GoToWebinar, it is reasonable.

From personal experience (and my own limited ability), these tools are all very self-explanatory. If you need additional help, you will find a huge range of tips on the internet, YouTube or, in the case of platforms like Remo and GoToWebinar, on their websites.

Activity	Tool	Apps/programmes
Virtual networking	Phone, tablet or PC	Remo, Zoom
Zoom activities	Phone, tablet or PC	Zoom, Teams
Online conferences	Tablet, PC	Remo
Phone calls	Phone	WhatsApp
Video calls	Phone, tablet or PC	Facetime, Zoom, Teams
Social media	Phone, tablet or PC	Relevant social media apps
Webinars	PC	GoToWebinar, Teams
Panel events/round tables	PC	Zoom, Teams
Videos	Phone, tablet	Video function in the camera app
Audio (including podcasts)	Phone	To record: voice memo app To edit: Audacity

Figure 2: What are the best tool and apps for each virtual BD activity?

Chapter 2: How to continue to develop your principal relationships virtually

In the first chapter we looked at the different ways to do virtual business development. These tips are pretty much applicable to delivering against all major business development objectives:

1. Boosting your profile in your chosen markets;
2. Creating new enquiries;
3. Putting you in front of people who could become your next new clients; and
4. Ensuring you stay visible to existing clients and contacts.

In this chapter I want to focus on the fourth objective on this list; making sure you stay visible to and continue to develop your principal working relationships.

Although it is last on this list, if I were going through a similar list in any other context it would be the first point. Why? Because the people you already work with (whether they are a client, introducer, or influencer) will always be your primary source of new work.

For many lawyers, business development is all about new client acquisition, which is odd as that is by far the hardest thing to do. Instead, my advice to our clients is always to flip the pyramid and invest the majority of your BD time and effort into getting more from the people you are already closest to.

In normal times, this isn't a big ask. You would probably be having meetings with your biggest clients in your offices or visiting them at theirs and punctuate the time in between with the occasional lunch or drinks.

You would probably have a similar system to manage your relationships with your main professional contacts, those who introduce new work or refer new clients to you. You may even have a co-marketing strategy in place that involves you hosting events or creating new content together.

However, how much have you been doing to ensure your most important relationships continue to develop while we have been unable to meet in person?

If you feel you could be doing more but are a little unsure as to what you should be doing or how to do it, I will use this chapter to share a simple structure (and some real life examples) that can be tweaked to suit any type of legal practice.

Create a list

The first part of any marketing campaign is to know who you want to talk to. Relationship development is no different. By far the easiest way to structure and manage your progress is to have a list that should include:

- Your most important clients (i.e. those who would leave a huge hole in your billings if they were to go to another firm);
- The clients you think should be spending more (whether in terms of offering you a larger share of their legal spend if they use several firms, or clients that only use you for one or two types of work when it's clear their needs extend beyond these);
- Your most productive introducers or referrers; and/or
- Your "key influencers" (the contacts you have who are particularly well connected within your primary target markets, i.e. the organizers of local business and/or networking groups, the executive staff within the relevant trade associations, journalists or prominent local businesspeople).

This list will probably include 10-15 names. If it is longer, you are not being selective enough. Remember, this is a qualitative exercise, so success is dependent on you focusing 80 percent of your business development efforts on the 20 percent of your clients and contacts who are responsible for 80 percent of your fee revenue.

Everyone else you are connected to can be taken care of using the other virtual marketing initiatives we've looked at, i.e. your blogs, articles, webinars and online events.

Have a plan

Once you have your list, the next step is to create a very simple development plan for each person on it. Usually I'd advocate an annual plan based on quarterly activities. I'd suggest you take a piece of paper and split it into quarters then write what you plan to do with each contact during each quarter into the relevant square so you always know where you are up to and what you need to do next.

However, as restrictions in different areas are continually changing, I think it is a much better idea to work in 30-day blocks across quarters. You want to stay flexible enough to adapt your plan according to what is and isn't permissible.

What does this mean in practice? It means splitting your list into thirds then assigning each third to one of the next three months. As my math isn't great, let's say your list is made up of 12 people. That means in month one you would concentrate on the first four, then the next four would be your targets for month two, and the remainder would be your focus for month three.

Once you know which contacts you need to contact in month one, you need to find a reason to make the initial contact to get your conversation started.

If you have "live" clients on your list, this will be fairly straightforward. You can ask for time to review a recently completed piece of work then broaden out that conversation to cover the client's future plans so you can identify where you may be able to help.

This help doesn't need to be limited to legal support. It may be that they are looking for land so you can offer to introduce them to one of your real estate contacts. They may need to value a business in which case you could offer to introduce them to an accountant you know who specializes in that type of work. Or it may be that they need services that another of the practice areas in your firm could help with, in which case you could offer to introduce them to the best qualified colleague.

If it is someone you haven't spoken to for a while – and this applies equally to clients and professional contacts – you need to find something that is relevant, recent, and interesting to use as an anchor. There are a number of ways of doing this:

- You can Google them to find their latest news;
- You can take a look at the news or updates page on their website;
- You can follow their social media posts; and/or
- You can sign up for Google alerts based on the name of their company or, if they are particularly prominent, your contact's name.

Once you find something that catches your eye, you can get in contact. The template we use (and feel free to edit this accordingly) is:

> *Hello [name],*
>
> *I wanted to get in touch because I have just seen you have [the subject area angle you have found]. It reminded me that it's been a while since we last spoke and I'd like to put that right and see if we can find a time to catch up. I'm very interested to find out more about [subject area]. I wondered if we could set up a video or phone call? Would [offer two dates and times] work? If not, please feel free to suggest a more convenient time and whether you prefer to talk on video or the phone and I'll send over an invite.*
>
> *I look forward to talking to you very soon.*

Again, giving your client or contact two date options makes it more likely that they will agree to one or come back with a third.

I know that sometimes the lawyers we work with can find it a little awkward to be so direct, but I'd like to offer three reassurances:

1. People are genuinely flattered that you are keeping up to date with their news, so the fact you have made mention of something that is important to them will get them onside.
2. If you have constructed your list properly, the person you will be emailing is someone who knows you well and someone you have history with, so all you are doing is facilitating the next step in your relationship. This is only "cold calling" when that history doesn't exist.
3. The majority of your contacts will be working from home too so they will welcome the chance to talk to someone different.

The last point is probably the most reassuring. While I've been trying to maintain my network during the past couple of months, not only have the people I've asked to catch up with accepted my invitations, I think every call has been longer and more involved than was originally planned.

Active listening

When I urge clients to engage in active listening during these calls, I sometimes encounter some incredulity. I'm told that of course they'll listen, why would you not listen when you are on a call?

But I'm not talking about just listening. I'm talking about *active* listening.

To better illustrate what I mean, let's start with the end in mind. The (business) reason you are having these calls is to kick start a process. Some call this process client relationship management (CRM) but I disagree. I very deliberately call it client development. To me, management is maintenance but development is growth, and surely the ultimate objective for any business (and every legal practice is very much a business) has to be growth?

During the call you need to identify the next step you will need to take to keep your conversation going, then at the end of the call:

- Tell your client or contact what you are going to do next;
- Tell them when you will do it by; and
- Then do what you said by when you said.

This is where the active listening comes in.

As you're speaking, try to note down anything you believe you can help with as it comes up in your conversations. With the main points in front of you on paper you can then revisit them later in the call by either asking for greater detail or offering potential solutions or support if it feels right to do so.

So what types of things could you listen out for? Here are a few examples from our recent client work:

- An email outlining how you would tackle a specific issue;
- Offering to provide a second opinion or external perspective on something of concern;
- A potential introduction to another client or to a colleague;
- Emailing them a link to a relevant article or a special report or white paper;
- Sharing the details of a group or event you discussed;
- An invitation to a webinar or online conference (organized by your firm or a third party); and
- Sharing something more personal, e.g. a restaurant recommendation or a recipe.

Keeping your conversations moving forward

Once you have a follow-up step agreed, the next stage is to deliver. But what happens after that? In some cases, the next step will present itself fairly immediately.

For example, if you had to send over a special report, the conversation could turn to finding the best way to get the messages it contains over to your client's wider team. This means you could offer an online training session to cover the legal aspects or implications of those messages.

Or, if you were making an introduction to another client, you would naturally follow up with both to see how their conversation went and ask if there is anything else you could do to help both parties progress their new association.

However, sometimes the next step won't present itself of its own accord. This is where some very simple objective-setting will help you massively. In fact, I'd suggest that you go through this exercise before you do any follow-up as you never know which conversations will organically yield a follow-up step and which won't.

Before you make your follow-up call, work out what you want from the conversation. The model we use is based on setting three clear objectives:

1. **Optimum** – what is the very best thing that could happen as a result of you speaking?
2. **Desired** – what would you like to happen as a result of you speaking?
3. **Essential** – what has to happen as a result of you speaking?

If we use the same two examples, your ODE objectives could be as follows.

1. Sending the special report

Essential – You have the opportunity to make sure it was received and can discuss how useful it was so that you can home in on the points that are most relevant to your client. This gives you a hook you can use to tee up your next conversation by sending over a link to a relevant blog or article.

Desired – Your conversation manages to highlight the main point of concern for the client and you can ask if they would be interested in some training on that point or a (branded) flowchart or "top tips" sheet

covering best practice that you can send over so your client's team can pin it up next to their desks as a reminder.
Optimum – The report not only highlights the client's main point of concern but also persuades them that action needs to be taken now and, as you're on the phone, that work goes to you there and then.

2. Making the introduction

Essential – Confirming the introduction led to a conversation between your two clients and you position yourself as ready, willing, and able to help if required. This allows you to leave your foot in the door and, if you make a diary note for four to six weeks hence, you can get back in touch to ask if anything has happened since you last spoke.
Desired – You find the conversation has taken place and there is a desire to do something together in the future but there could be few things you may be required to smooth over to facilitate that joint venture. You would then ask about timeframes and again put a marker in your diary to go back for an update at the point your client has suggested.
Optimum – The introductory conversation went well and there is an immediate need or legal advice to progress your clients' joint plans.

Initially, this may look like more work, but let me assure you, if setting your ODE objectives is taking you longer than five minutes and involves more than a pen and a post-it note, you are over-investing!

If you follow these steps you will be having regular and credible conversations with your main clients and contacts. But instead of leaving those conversations with a "very nice to speak to you, we must do it again soon", you'll be leaving with that all important next follow-up step already in place.

Most importantly, you will be initiating a process rather than just holding disjointed one-off conversations. Process is what you need if your conversations are going to take you to your ultimate objective – new work.

How do you remain visible virtually between your planned meetings?

While the video and phone calls are the parts of your development plans that will yield the results, there are a few things you can do to maintain your visibility between your planned conversations.

This is an essential part of the process. Your clients and contacts need to have continual reminders that you are not only still there but also still involved with the types of work they associate with you. However, all of these tips are incredibly time-efficient and can all be done virtually from your phone:

- Like and share their posts on LinkedIn;
- Like and share their tweets;
- If you have Google alerts on your contacts, use their good news as updates on your own social media feeds alongside a short congratulatory message;
- If you see your clients mentioned in the press, send them the link with a relevant supporting email;
- If you publish any written, video, or audio content that is relevant to them, send an email alerting them to it with an email cover note explaining why you're sending it;
- If you are running any online events or webinars that would be beneficial to your contacts, send them an invite (your main marketing drive could well have been missed);
- If you see something in the trade or local press that may be useful to your clients, send them the link or PDF (if it is in hard copy, cut it out and mail it – that is even more flattering); and
- Returning to the personal aspect, if there is anything in the press or on TV or radio that you know would be of interest, send your clients the link.

All of these things show you are looking out for your most important clients and contacts, and that you are invested in a long-term working relationship, not just the next piece of work. Time and time again we are told how important this is when we interview our clients' clients as part of their independent client listening campaigns.

> *"I want them to tell me what I don't know."*

> *"I want to know they are always looking out for me."*

> *"I need to know they are on top of the things that affect me."*

This is, in the client or introducer's eyes, the real added value of working with you.

Of course, if you make sure you add a line at the bottom of your email that reminds them you are available to discuss anything related to the links you've sent in more detail, it will immediately become the most targeted piece of marketing you do that day.

I will not pretend there are any hard and fast rules as to how quickly this type of activity will convert into work, but I will make one promise. Adopting this more structured approach to client development will prove your commitment to your clients. It will help you make sure your primary relationships are intact once things do start to go back to the next phase of normality.

Would this happen anyway? Perhaps, but people are nervous at the moment; they need reassurance that you are in their corner and willing to provide the additional support they need while things are unfamiliar, uncertain, and unpredictable. If you are not providing that reassurance regularly, they could well look elsewhere.

Better still, this will not involve an enormous amount of time or effort. All of this can be done virtually by telephone, video call, and email, and fitted in around your billable work while we can't get out and see our main clients and contacts in person.

Chapter 3:
How to penetrate new markets virtually

In the previous chapter we looked at what you need to do to continue to develop your most likely source of new work – the people you know best. While this is much easier than new client acquisition, this doesn't mean that you can't find new clients while you're working remotely. However, as with all of your other business development, the current environment just means it needs to be done a little differently.

Step one: Focus

If you do want to pursue new markets, the first step has to be to decide on the areas you want to focus on. The reason for this is if you set out with a scattergun approach, trying to reach every potential client by all means necessary, you will end up spending a lot of time (and potentially a lot of money) without accomplishing very much at all. You will spread yourself too thin and as a result you will never achieve critical mass in any particular market.

Instead, you need to start by working out who would make the best new clients for your practice. For lawyers who advise businesses (corporate, commercial, employment, commercial property) this means picking particular industry sectors. When you're choosing your sectors, the golden rule is to use the terminology your clients use, not the terminology traditionally employed by law firms. For example, no business describes itself as an SME or an Owner Managed Business. Your clients will describe themselves as a technology business, a farm, a retailer, or a manufacturer. This means these are the types of words you should be using while you develop your focus.

If you are a lawyer who provides services to individuals, you could either target defined geographic areas, or home in on particular demographics within your local market. For example, if your local area has a large German population, this could be your target. Or if you have particularly affluent zip codes in your local area or if your town is surrounded by huge amounts of agricultural land or is home to a large military or naval base, these could become your focus.

The main benefit of applying this level of focus is, once you know exactly who you are speaking to, you can start to tailor your messaging to the exact requirements of your audience. You will be able to communicate using the correct language, the most relevant points of reference, and the latest headlines. When you do this, you will position yourself as one of them, someone they feel comfortable talking to, rather than just another lawyer looking to leverage work from them.

This alone will increase the productivity of your business development efforts. You will immediately become a more attractive option than those competitors who are still convinced that marketing themselves as generalists is the only option.

Step two: Create your "murder wall"

This phrase may take you by surprise (it is certainly one that tends to grab the attention of even the least marketing-friendly lawyers while we are helping them put their plans together) so let me explain.

If you think about crime dramas on TV, the camera often cuts away to a wall covered in photographs, notes, arrows, and other clues. This is the "murder wall" the detectives are using to piece together every aspect of the crime. It is the visual representation that will help them to unravel the clues and achieve their objective – to catch the killer.

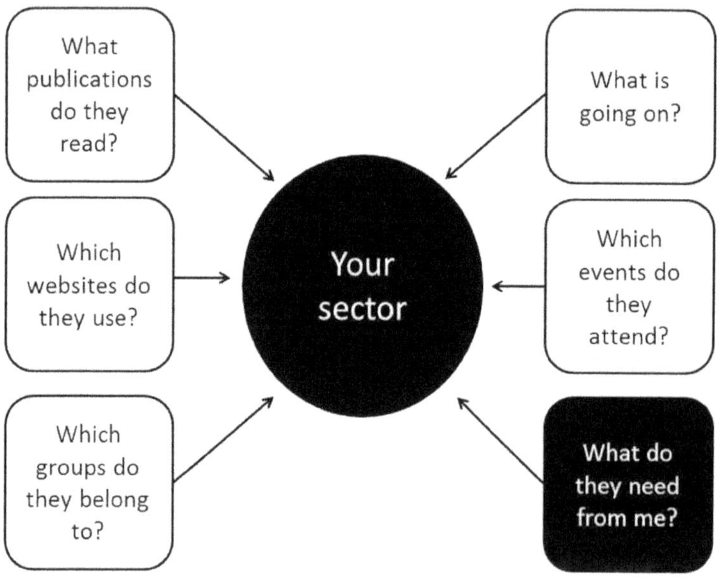

Figure 3: The "murder wall".

This is the approach we'd suggest you take. It provides a visual representation of all the potential routes into your chosen market and sets out all the different types of information you should be looking to assemble.

I'd like to look at each of these headings in a little more detail.

What publications do they read?

Probably the easiest way to examine the publications part is to again divide practice areas into those for businesses and those for individuals. With businesses, you will be looking at the trade press. Every sector has at least one dedicated publication and, believe me, having worked extensively with intellectual property lawyers for years, I can confidently say there are no exceptions, however niche you go.

Once you know the relevant titles, you can approach the editors with ideas for editorial. The fact you will be approaching your piece from a legal angle will be attractive to the editor as it will give their contents page a little more diversity and their readers a wider perspective.

With individuals, you will more likely be looking at the local press. Which newspapers, magazines, and community free press are produced in your local area? Who is responsible for editing the news?

Once you have these details you can contact them to let them know you would be willing to produce editorial for their readers on the topics of interest to them, or make yourself available for comment should a story with a legal aspect come up.

In more usual times, I would always suggest you invite members of the local press to your hospitality events. As that is not possible at the moment, another way to position yourself as a potential legal commentator could be to disagree with something that their publication has printed. This may seem a little mischievous, but as long as you politely explain why you don't agree with the particular point and offer to produce a response, the editor can publish "in order to give their readers a more comprehensive and balanced view", and it can sometimes be enough to start a new conversation.

There are of course possible overlaps between the trade and local press. For example, if your local newspaper has a regular business feature, you may want to be seen in that so you reach local businesses. Or – going back to the German community idea – there may be a national publication that goes out to all of the German-speaking communities in your country.

Producing editorial is a hugely effective way to reach a new audience. It also means you reach them, having already been positioned as an expert (after all, why would the editor have asked you to write or comment if you weren't an expert?). This is a position that a paid-for ad or a sponsored "advertising feature" will never command.

It is also free – apart from your time – which is something your management board will appreciate. Better yet, if your offer of editorial is accepted and you meet their brief and deliver on time, the chances are you will continue to receive intermittent invitations to write again.

Which websites do they use?

This follows on from the previous point. For many sectors (in particular science- and technology-led sectors) websites will be the principal point of reference. Just as magazines need articles, websites need more new content as they are continually updated. This means your offer of an article or blog will probably be snapped up even more readily.

As websites are consumed visually you can also be a little more creative with formats. As well as traditional written content you can offer infographics and "talking head" videos. As you will already be producing this type of content having read chapter one of this book, you will already have the content ready to roll, which will make the whole process easier and more efficient for you. Many websites also now run their own podcasts, so offering to appear as a guest is also an option.

The great thing about providing website content is everything you publish will have a link you can share via social media. If you tag the website and the journalist you worked with into your posts, this will introduce you to all of their followers, which again will extend your market reach.

Which groups do they belong to?

If we again use the business/individual divider, for industry sectors you will probably be looking for trade bodies and independent professional networks. For more local targets you will probably be looking for less formal groups, including networking groups and clubs based on personal interests.

For me, trade bodies are one of the most forgotten and underrated business development opportunities. Not only will all their members be prospective clients but:

- All their professional affiliate members could be potential referrers;
- All trade bodies have newsletters and websites that need content;
- All will have some form of educational program for their members that need speakers;

- All will have social media presences that you can participate in; and
- Once we can meet again, all will have regular conferences and/or social events that you will (eventually) be able to join in with so you can meet their members in person.

Another type of group you can join while we're working remotely is LinkedIn groups.

These have rather lost the luster they had in the early days of LinkedIn because they have become flooded with sales messages rather than discussions. However, there are still exceptions so it is always worth a quick search in case your chosen sectors are amongst the good ones.

Although local networking groups and clubs have obviously been affected by the current restrictions, almost all have used the types of video platforms we looked at earlier to keep their memberships in touch. This means it is still worth searching what is available and operational.

Depending on where you are, one type of group that seems to have been less affected is sports clubs. Like trade bodies, these are all too often overlooked as a business development option, especially as some lawyers just don't associate sports and hobbies with BD. However, if your local area is your target market, sports clubs provide a great way to get to know a number of local people. Moreover, as you will all be doing something you genuinely enjoy, it doesn't even feel like networking! This is something I know that many lawyers we work with really appreciate.

At the moment there is one additional way to involve yourself and your practice with your local area.

Because parts of your community will have been affected more seriously by the current crisis, there may be certain aid and support initiatives you could get involved with. Again, this will provide you with a chance to work more closely with local people from all walks of life and give you the opportunity to underline just how committed you are to your community.

Which events do they attend?

This is obviously the trickiest part, but you shouldn't disregard events altogether, especially as they will restart at some point. With that in mind, I'd suggest you complete this part of the puzzle by researching two things:

1. Which networking events and conferences are being run online? You can then sign up to (and, of course, participate in) the ones that are.

2. Which are the major events in your sector or region? Can you register your interest now so you receive the details as soon as they restart?

What is going on?

It is almost impossible to talk about current issues if you are not completely up to date with them. This means you need to keep a continual watching brief on the latest news. If you have completed the website and publications part of the "murder wall" process, this will be easy. These two media will send you updates on the news and developments from across your sector or region. If you want to supplement those feeds, you can also set up Google alerts using the relevant keywords.

However, there is one more source of information open to you and, if you get this one right, you could actually win work while you're using it; your clients and contacts.

If we go back to the previous chapter and align your shortlist of key clients with your new business focus, you will be speaking to clients and professional contacts within your areas of focus. By extension, they can become your primary source of news, insight, and gossip.

What do they need from me?

By this stage of the process you will know how your sector or region is made up, the types of businesses and/or individuals involved, what is going on, and the issues they are most likely to face. Now you need to be able to explain exactly how your legal specialisms will help them tackle these issues. That is what they need from you.

This should be a very straightforward exercise, but if you are a visual person one suggestion I often make when I get to this stage with clients is to take a piece of paper and draw a line down the middle. Then, on the left you list the key issues your market faces and, on the right, what you can do to resolve those issues.

Admittedly, there is a lot to cover here so if you have a marketing function in your firm, I'd suggest enlisting their help. Not only will they give you the additional resource you need but as you will also undoubtedly need their help when it comes to implementing your plans, having them onboard and up to speed already will cut a huge corner further down the line. Alternatively, you could enlist the help of one or two willing colleagues. This takes us neatly to the next step; putting all your market insight into action.

Step three: Action

Once you know who you are targeting and how you get your message out to them, the next step is to actually put those two things together. Many people try to make marketing far more complicated than it actually is. Marketing people love initialisms, acronyms, and buzzwords and this peculiar (and unnecessary) language tends to put non-marketers off. Instead, I'd urge you to think about what marketing really is.

If you were to take a piece of paper and draw two circles at either side then write "what I have" in one and "who needs it" in the other, then draw a line between the two circles, that line is marketing. Marketing is simply the vehicle that takes what you have to who needs to buy it.

This is why the "murder wall" exercise is so important. It will show you what your line needs to be made up of – the publications, websites, speaking slots, online events, new contacts, trade bodies, and networking groups that will allow you to set out what you do in front of the people who need it.

But how do you turn that static line into an active flow of information from you to your target markets?

The first thing I would do is to choose a few colleagues you like working with. Working as a team always helps. At the most practical level, more hands make lighter work. However, having a team also provides cover for when one member has their BD time overtaken by fee-earning work so progress can continue.

As we're all human beings, it's actually nice to have the support and encouragement of our co-workers. This point takes us back to that first (and arguably most important) selection criterion. Yes, of course you need to include at least one person to represent all of the different practice areas your target market needs, but you also all need to get on.

As we are all working remotely, at least for the majority of the time, you need to stay in touch and provide each other with updates, ideas, and introductions – virtually. That job immediately becomes harder, if deep down, you feel you don't really want to talk to the other parties in your team.

But there is one final selection criteria to bear in mind. Good business development involves four personality types – the networker, the writer, the speaker, and the researcher. Very few people possess all of these skills, so finding the right blend across your team will maximize your chances of success.

In summary, while you're choosing your team you need to find a combination of people who:

- You get on with;
- Represent all of the required practice areas; and
- Are able to provide you with networking, writing, presenting, and research skills.

Step four: What gets measured gets done

Once you have your team, you need a plan and that will involve you meeting. Hopefully, this can be done onsite but if that is still an impossibility, you can use Teams or Zoom.

This first meeting would be used to determine who will be responsible for:

- Maintaining a watching brief on the news (and circulating what they find);
- Writing new content for the firm's website and social media channels;
- Identifying and signing up for any relevant online events;
- Identifying and initiating contact with the relevant trade bodies and/or networking or interest groups;
- Identifying and initiating contact with the relevant publications and websites; and
- Setting the next meeting so you can update each other on your progress.

At subsequent meetings, the actions will be discussed and next steps will be recorded so you can tick those off as you go. More importantly, you can start to track the new contacts you have made and the new conversations that have begun as a result, again using the same model set out for client/contact development set out in the previous chapter.

In our experience, adding this additional layer of personal accountability and structure is what ensures things actually happen. You will be able to track progress in terms of the increase in:

- Self-published blogs and articles;
- External editorial opportunities you've won;
- The online events you've participated in;
- The webinars, round tables, or panel events you've run;

- The new marketing opportunities your contacts within the trade bodies and networking groups have introduced;
- The new contacts you've made;
- The new opportunities your conversations with these contacts have led to; and
- Eventually, the new work and new fees your efforts have generated.

Chapter 4:
Practical planning – how to create an effective 30-day plan

As things are fluid at the moment, my advice would be to concentrate on the next 30 days rather than looking any further ahead.

This will allow you to maintain a higher degree of flexibility so you can switch from virtual to physical business development as and when your local restrictions change. Operating within this shorter timescale allows you to switch back again if required.

The template overleaf is designed to help you plan your BD activities for the month ahead in a simple format you can refer back to and update as you need to.

It covers all of the major BD disciplines – client development, networking, writing, presenting, and other media – and can incorporate all of the different virtual BD vehicles we looked at in chapter one. But that definitely doesn't mean every box needs to be filled.

As with all business development, you will always achieve the best results by concentrating on the activities that suit you best and are most relevant to your practice.

To give you a better idea, on the page after the template there is a working example (using a manufacturing sector focus) of how a completed plan could look.

Name:
Period:

Objective	In person	In writing	Events	Presentations	Other
Client development					
Professional contacts					
New client acquisition					

Figure 4: The 30-day plan template.

Name: J Doe
Period: January 2021

Objective	In person	In writing	Events	Presentations	Other
Client development	Video calls with: • XYZ Manufacturing Ltd • 123 Fabrications • New Tech Inc.			Commercial contract video training session for Iron and Steel LLP	
Professional contacts			Virtual team-on-team drinks with 1st State Bank		Podcast with ABC Accountants
New client acquisition		New blogs: • Current M&A trends in the manufacturing industry • How to maximise your business value at exit		Host manufacturing round table event	Chase editor of *Manufacturing Today* re. proposed article

Figure 5: An example of a 30-day plan.

Part 2:
Refresh

Chapter 5:

Adapt, improvise, overcome – adopting a more flexible approach to marketing and BD

If someone were to assess Clint Eastwood's incredible back catalogue, it is highly unlikely that 1986's *Heartbreak Ridge* would merit even a minor mention. However, although it's far from his best work, the film does contain a line that has over the years become a bit of a business development mantra for us:

> *"Adapt, improvise, overcome."*

If business development is going to be successful, it has to be underpinned by structure and process. But this doesn't mean it is an exact science. It doesn't matter how strong your message is, how methodical you are in terms of your personal approach and follow up, or how slick your comms, content, and social media are – you are still marketing to people and people are, by definition, erratic and unpredictable.

This means that sometimes you will have to tweak what you are doing. You will need to adapt and improvise as you go if you are going to overcome the inevitable obstacles and achieve your ultimate objective – to win work.

While the need to adapt, improvise, and overcome has (or should have) always been a necessary part of every firm's approach to marketing and business development, it is even more crucial today. Up until now too many law firms have been happy continuing to market the way they always have. This really isn't a criticism. In my experience it is never done out of anything more sinister than misguided inertia.

However, with everything in a heightened state of flux, doing what we have always done is no longer an option.

You may have heard the phrase, "insanity is doing the same thing over and over again and expecting different results". It has been credited to everyone from Albert Einstein to George Bernard Shaw and Samuel Beckett but, to be honest, its source is unimportant. I only use it to elucidate a point.

In the past, law firms could do the same things over and over again in the hope that different results would achieved. This is because the differences were marginal – sometimes the same marketing activities generated good results, sometimes they achieved mediocre results, and sometimes the results weren't that great... but they did achieve *some* results so we kept on doing them.

The only problem is the major variable in all of these experiments – the world and more specifically the way we now have to live and work – has now altered beyond recognition.

I have tried hard to steer away from using the word "unprecedented" because all of us are tired of seeing, hearing, and reading that word. But like all clichés it has become so because it is true. None of us have ever lived through times like these and, hand on heart, I hope none of us ever have to again.

From a commercial perspective we have nothing to compare or refer back to in terms of how best to market during these conditions, and we don't know what's going to happen and when. This means we now have to be prepared to apply a far greater degree of flexibility than ever before.

This need for flexibility and continual adaptation and improvisation isn't a temporary measure.

None of us have any real idea of how the working world will look when we get through the next few months, so the need to adapt and improvise will continue to play a vital role in ensuring we enjoy a successful commercial future.

My challenge to you is how to imbed a more flexible BD culture now. How do you make sure that you and your colleagues know how to ride change and use it to your benefit?

In the last chapter, the word "flexibility" was used quite a lot, but more in terms of altering tactics to meet the changing restrictions. In this chapter I want to take that one stage further. I want to look at the strategic value of flexibility and how being ready and able to consistently adapt, improvise, and overcome will generate better results than staying flat-footed.

What are your non-negotiables?

Perhaps the best place to start is to look at what *can't* be adapted. I like to call these your non-negotiables; these are the building blocks of your practice and address the fundamental reasons your clients come to you.

These will of course vary from lawyer to lawyer and from firm to firm but I'd suggest that the list would look something like this:

1. Your proposition

Or to give it its full name, your client value proposition (CVP).

This is basically your core sales message. It should crystallize what you do, how you do it, and, most importantly, spell out why how you do what you do adds real benefit to your clients.

Your CVP is the answer you would give to the question, "So, why should I work with you?"

Good marketing demands consistency. You need to have a concrete proposition that all of your fee earners can understand and articulate clearly in their own words in any situation. Your CVP should be front and center on your website and in your marketing materials and pitch documents.

It should also be identifiable in your blogs and articles. For example, if you are positioning yourselves as clear, practical, and commercial, does your content clearly lay out practical solutions that will help your clients adopt and maintain a more commercial focus?

While your marketing channels may change, your core marketing message can't. However you get your message to market (and however that approach needs to be adapted and improvised), you cannot afford to do anything that would dent or confuse your proposition.

2. Your target markets

Once you focus in on a specific market, you need to commit to these targets long-term. Marketing doesn't work overnight. Just because you don't see an immediate financial return doesn't mean you have chosen the wrong sectors. It takes time and trial and error to permeate a market. It also takes tenacity.

As long as you have chosen your sectors based on your specialisms, your experience, your interests and your belief that they offer either growth or long-term stability, you just need to find the right way to get in. And that is the bit that will undoubtedly require you to adapt and improvise as you go.

3. Your personal brand

A personal brand is admittedly another marketing-ism but it is important, especially in terms of your personal business development.

The term refers to the way you are perceived and recognized in your market; the impression you leave on people once you've met them. It tends to be made up of a combination of experience, expertise, competencies, actions and/or achievements. It also highlights the way you operate in terms of approach and service.

While there is a school of thought that personal brand can be adapted to different situations, I disagree. Clients want genuine. If you are seen to be reinventing yourself repeatedly the sense of you being a genuine person is easily damaged.

Marketing is always as much about who you don't want to work with as who you do want to work with. So, while your style won't work for some, it will connect with the rest of your market. This is the half you should be concentrating on and for the other half, you will undoubtedly have a colleague that will be more to their liking.

4. Your fundamental service values

I remember a few years ago a senior partner in an intellectual property practice told me that his clients never know if he's doing a good job at the time, they only know if they have been properly looked after. While I disagree with the first half of that story (especially these days because clients tend to be much better informed as to what good work looks like), I certainly agree with the second half.

People want service, and any suggestion that you are anything short of totally focused on each client while you're working with them can cause them to question the longevity of your working relationship. Even if they stay with you because it's an easier option than moving, a lack of service will impact on your business development. Poor service is the easiest way to destroy your potential referral rate.

Moreover, personal service levels are always mentioned when we interview our clients' clients during their client listening programs.

There is also an argument that this area is even more important given the majority of our meetings are going to be virtual and via video. You no longer have the opportunity to dazzle clients with your front of house experience or your meeting rooms. This means you have to follow the golden rules:

- When you are in a video meeting, make sure your client is your only focus. Don't get caught reading another screen, tapping on-screen notifications or being distracted by your phone.
- Turn up to your meetings on time. In fact, turn up five minutes early in case your client is early. The last thing they want to do is wait in a virtual waiting room until you are able to arrive.
- Although you are at a desk at home, the same rules apply to virtual meetings as they do to office meetings. Look smart, don't start eating, be ready to take notes and have the relevant supporting paperwork to hand (or emails up on a separate screen).

- Confirm next steps and make sure they are completed by the deadline you set.

What can you adapt, improvise, and overcome?

Now we know what we can't change, let's take a look at what we can.

The starting point is to know what needs to be changed. This will involve monitoring and measurement. This need not be a labor- or time-intensive process; it simply requires you to remain aware of how your various business development activities are working.

Video/phone calls with clients

Are these generating the level of new opportunities, introductions, and insight they should be? Are you achieving the objectives you've set yourself ahead of the call? Are you leaving with (and completing) the follow-up steps you need to keep your conversations moving forward?

If the answer is yes, maybe you could look at extending your list and increase the likelihood of creating even more new opportunities. Or you could look at your firm's wider client list to identify some potential cross-selling targets. If you find some, you can ask the relevant colleague to introduce you so you can start to develop these relationships alongside your own.

If the answer is no, it is time to examine why they're not generating the results you'd expected and adapt your approach accordingly. From experience the usual reasons client calls don't work include the following:

The calls aren't being scheduled because your email invitations are going ignored

This means you need to change the way you schedule your calls. Maybe you could call their assistant to fix the meeting or even call unannounced. As said earlier, this probably wouldn't work in more normal times but while we're working remotely your call could well be welcomed as it'll add some needed variety to your client's day.

You are leaving the call without an agreed follow-up step

Although your calls are doubtlessly very friendly, if no follow-up steps are agreed, the conversation can't progress. This means you need to invest more heavily in planning your calls.

You haven't quite got round to it because of work pressures

This is the easiest one to address. Your plan will never generate results if it's not put into action. Take a leaf out of Nike's book and just do it!

Video/phone calls with professional contacts

All of the previous points apply to calls with your professional contacts but there are two other factors to consider.

Are you avoiding the tough questions?

Sometimes people can feel awkward asking for an introduction or an opportunity to meet more of your contacts' colleagues or members. It feels too salesy, too direct. Please don't worry about this. As long as you have a reason for asking for the introduction, the majority of your requests will be accepted. Better still, if you have something pre-prepared that you can offer in return, that could make it even easier.

Are your requests being refused?

If your joint marketing suggestions are being refused or ignored, try to come up with more creative ideas or just ask them what they would like to do and fit in with their preferences. Once you have gone along with one of their ideas, the unwritten rules of reciprocity should kick in and your next suggestion should be met positively.

Virtual events

This is arguably the easiest activity to monitor because you will know by the attendance figures how popular your chosen approach is proving. Let the data show you what's working, what you need to do more of, and what you shouldn't be doing at all.

The types of trends to look for include:

- Are social or educational events proving most popular?
- Are traditional webinars or more interactive formats proving most popular?
- Of the alternative formats, which are pulling the largest audiences?
- Are there particular topics that create higher levels of interest?
- Are there different trends for different practice areas?
- If "live" attendance is down, what are the viewing figures like when you post the sessions on your website or on YouTube?

Once you have this data to hand you can start to adapt your approach so that you are using the right formats and delivery mechanisms for each practice area and focusing on tackling the subjects of greatest interest.

Blogs

The monitoring process is very similar to that required for events. You need to identify which topics and which formats (whether those are written, e.g. top tips, FAQs, short form or long form, or more fundamental, e.g. the difference between written, video, animation, and audio) create the highest levels of engagement.

Similarly, you may want to look at your headings. However strong your content is, your heading is what makes people click. Are you generating better results from using questions via a "clickbait" approach (i.e. "Six ways you can minimize the potential for a contractual dispute") or are the headings that borrow from the news or popular culture drawing the biggest audience?

Again, you need to monitor across practice areas as there may be a difference between the ways different markets want to consume your information. For example, a young tech business will probably prefer shorter online video content while an older wills and probate client will probably want to see things written down in short and easy to digest steps.

Perhaps a less obvious factor to monitor is tone of voice. Are you generating a larger reaction when you use an informative tone, or a friendly, more informal, tone?

Social media

Social media is actually quite hard to measure. You can (and definitely should) look at click through rates and views, shares, and likes as they will give you a pretty accurate idea of:

- What catches your audience's eye;
- The topics of greatest interest; and
- The tone of voice or structure that makes the most popular posts.

It will also give you an idea as to what time of day works best for the different parts of your target market. If we use the tech and "silver surfer" examples again, it is likely the tech clients will start later in the morning so posting first thing is unlikely to reach them. Meanwhile, your older clients are more likely to be online at different points during the day so you will need to monitor engagement to assess when the best time is to reach them.

With regards to how you adapt your approach, this data will give you some prompts on topic, tone, and timing, but – and this is why I say social media is hard to measure – it will only tell you half the story. It will not tell you who is following you at a distance, and who keeps up with your latest news as they scroll through their timelines.

This means you can't capture what it is that they like about your posts because they don't interact with them – even though it is this part of your following that could very well yield your next client.

When do you need to adapt, improvise, and overcome?

Although it's admittedly not my sport, I do remember the inimitable and highly quotable New England coach Bill Belichick once saying he never waits until half time to make changes because you can see everything you need to from the first plays. Business development is no different.

If you can see response dropping or certain things working better than others, make the changes there and then.

You only have a finite amount of time for business development because your raison d'etre is to look after your clients, your practice, and your billings. This means you need to focus the time you do have on the things you need to work, and if they aren't working to the levels you'd expect, you need to adapt, improvise, and overcome.

And this takes us straight back to the Einstein (or Shaw, or Beckett) quote. Why would you keep doing the same things expecting a different result? More to the point, why would you keep investing time, budget, and effort to do the same things expecting a different result?

You wouldn't do it in any other aspect of your life so don't do it in business development! Instead, be ready to adapt, improvise, and overcome.

Chapter 6: Formulating a personal BD plan that combines the best of the old with the best of the new

As time goes on, the restrictions will change and your business development plan will need to change with them.

However, while there will be an opportunity to reintroduce more traditional business development activities, it is also essential that we continue to employ some of the new approaches we've utilized to such good effect during whilst working virtually. This is especially important as it is highly likely that anything other than meeting in small groups is still some way off.

The need to create hybrid business development plans that combine the best of the old with the best of the new is not solely driven by market factors. There is also profitability to consider.

Publishing content, running online events, keeping in contact via video and making greater use of social media come at a fraction of the cost of physical BD; you don't have venue or catering costs, nor do you have to pay for travel (and that includes the billable hours lost while you're in a car or on a train or plane) or client entertainment.

There is also the potential size of the audience you can reach virtually to consider.

The cost per lead or enquiry generated by your virtual activities is always going to be markedly less than it would be if you were solely dependent on creating opportunities at conferences or networking or social events. It is also arguable that the number of new contacts you make will be higher given you can be more targeted in your preparation for an online event. This will reduce the gamble that you will just happen upon the people you want to meet (or not meet them at all if you're unlucky).

With that in mind, for the next few months at least, the key to successfully marrying the old and the new will be our ability to draw a line between business development and marketing.

If we use the most straightforward definitions, "business development" refers to activities that involve you talking one on one with a particular person. "Marketing" refers to activities that allow you to talk to your market/s as a whole. So, with that in mind it is probably not too much of a generalization to say the reintroduction of the old can be your business development activities and the newer ideas you want to retain can be your marketing.

How do you manage the reintroduction of the best of the old?

If you have been managing your key relationships, moving video and phone calls to meeting in person should be a natural progression. As we've already discussed, the most important thing to remember while you make the transition is to maintain your emotional intelligence.

Everyone has a different attitude towards their personal risk, and different people will have had different direct experience of the impact of the virus. This means you need to ask everyone you invite for a meeting if they are comfortable meeting in person or if they would prefer to continue to meet virtually for the time being at least.

An intermediary step is to offer to meet either at your offices or at your clients' or contacts' premises. As all businesses have had to undergo a COVID assessment, there is often a higher degree of reassurance that the meeting environment will be safer. This is particularly going to be the case if you meet at your clients' premises because they will know exactly what has been done to ensure your safety whilst onsite.

That said, invitations for lunch may also be enthusiastically received, as long, of course, as you pick a venue you know has been fastidious in their adherence to the relevant guidelines.

As with all business development, the answer is to know your client and play to their preferences without compromising on both parties' personal safety.

Although reinstating face time with your "A list" is obviously the priority in terms of reintroducing old style BD, the next most important group to focus on is the people you met through your business development. You may have come across them at an online conference or networking event. They may have responded to a piece of content they found. Or, they may have simply caught your eye, having engaged with your social media.

In more normal times you would probably have invited these new contacts to either an educational or hospitality event and made sure you had an opportunity to talk. This would have given you the perfect bridge to getting back in touch afterwards to invite them for breakfast, lunch, or coffee so you could pick up on a particular point and discuss it in more depth. At the moment we have to be a little more bullish and go straight to the coffee stage.

Having said that, I do still maintain you have to push any new contact through the two-question filter process:

1. Are they potentially useful contacts?
2. Did I like them?

Again, if you get two yeses then the fact you have invited them to meet one-on-one should not only be understandable, it should also be met with a fast and positive response.

Aside from (or, perhaps, instead of) moving your face-to-face meetings back in to your personal BD plan as soon as restrictions reduce, there is one other initiative I'd urge you to consider. Client listening.

I have mentioned client listening in passing several times earlier on in the book but I'd like to look at it in a little more detail here.

I know I don't need to explain the concept as it is something most law firms now do in some form. It is simply the process of engaging someone to interview your clients to find out how they see your working relationship. They will find out what is good (and you can use this part of the feedback to inform your marketing choices and strengthen your service offering), what needs attention, and what else you could be doing for the client.

The listening process offers immeasurable benefits. It allows you to underline your commitment to providing the highest possible level of service for your clients, which on its own will generate immeasurable trust and goodwill. It is also pretty much self-funding. As you will be asking what else you could be doing for each client, they will literally be finding their own cross-selling opportunities for you to progress with them.

You will have noticed I suggested you engage someone external to do the interviewing. This is sometimes where I can be challenged. Lawyers will ask me why a colleague – or more specifically their senior or managing partners – can't conduct the interviews. Up to a point they are right. They are more than capable and will have a greater understanding of the history of the relationship than someone brought in from the outside.

However, what they don't have is independence.

The fact they have the firm's name on their business card can often cause clients to hold back and, even if it's only by degrees, the exercise will not uncover everything it should. The missing piece could be the crucial one.

My other argument is that when you utilize someone who is used to running this type of campaign, they know from experience when people are holding back and require a little more (gentle) probing. Again, we could only be talking degrees but as the interviewee displays signs of discomfort, the chances are that what they are not saying is just as important as what they are.

The reason I mention client listening now is that, with things as they are, it is entirely likely that your clients could need a very different type of support from you.

From a business perspective their plans, market, or lives could have changed dramatically since March 2020. This means they could now require your immediate help with something specific or an introduction to one of your colleagues or contacts.

From a more practical perspective, the way they work may have changed over the last year. This could mean they have very different service delivery demands, demands that you could implement for your other clients in similar circumstances to strengthen your relationships and give you a more competitive offering to take to market.

We will look at how to make best use of this type of feedback in the next chapter.

Client listening also gives you an easy way back into any client relationships that may have stalled because of social distancing or the pure challenge of operating under the current circumstances.

Each interview will provide you with clear follow-up steps and, because the suggestions will have come straight from the horse's mouth, your clients will be expecting you to take them. This means there should be no reticence on your part to reconnect, pick up the reins, and kick start your working relationship back into life.

Most of all, you need to remember the personal aspect. Your clients need to know you are there for them, now more than ever.

You don't need me to tell you that these are hugely uncertain times and getting through them intact could well require us to approach things in both our personal and private lives in very different ways.

While we make the next round of decisions as to what we will need to do differently to combat our current challenges, the value of the support from and counsel of our professional advisers will be paramount.

This means you need to let your clients know in no uncertain terms that you remain accessible, responsive, and ready to provide advice or the external, impartial, opinions they will undoubtedly need over the coming months.

How do you retain the best of the new?

If you are tracking the performance of your content, your virtual events, and your social media, you will already know what works for you, your practice, and your audience, so the choices as to what you need to retain will be easy to make.

However, there are other critical success factors:

- Virtual marketing is more profitable;
- Virtual marketing potentially provides you with a broader reach; and
- It is highly unlikely large-scale events will return any time soon.

There is actually a case to be made that very little has to change. The smartest move will be to continue to publish content (both on your website/social media and in the trade or local press), keep your events online, and maintain an active yet targeted presence on social media.

Keeping these activities going while you are trying to reintroduce meetings in person could, however, be difficult, so here are four alternative strategies that may help reduce the burden on you or the group you have been working on.

1. Seek more collaborative options internally

As I said earlier in the book, when it comes to business development, working in teams is always best. It means you have a Plan B, a backstop in case the time you thought you had for business development suddenly disappears under a pile of work. Similarly, it means you can step in if one of your colleagues is suddenly required to drop everything for an influx of new matters.

If you haven't created a team around you by this point, it may be worth revisiting that and starting to put one together. It will allow you to divide activities between more pairs of hands, which will make it easier to cover all bases while you have your hands full with client work and reintroducing the face-to-face business development you know you need to do.

Alternatively, you could look at your chosen markets and see which additional legal areas your clients also need updates from. If there are some, why not ask your colleagues in those departments if they could come up with any ideas for articles, blogs, or webinars for your audience?

For example, if you have been providing M&A updates to help your clients take full advantage of the keen pricing that market uncertainty can cause, you could ask your colleagues in the employment department to provide a follow-up session. They could explain how best to manage the onboarding process for the new employees who would have arrived as a result of recent acquisitions.

2. Seek more collaborative options externally

As your face-to-face meeting schedule will include your main professional contacts, you could take the opportunity to ask them if they are planning any marketing initiatives you could be a part of. This would at least reduce your admin and organizational time. It may even provide more of a focus so you only have to produce the required output rather than spend time coming up with ideas.

Or you could ask them if they would be interested in producing a guest blog or hosting a session/producing a video as part of your current legal update series. If they are willing, all you would need to do is post or publish their material so you can continue to keep your name in front of the audience you have built up with the minimum of effort.

3. Delegate down

Depending on where you are in your career and the current situation within your firm, you may be able to delegate your content and social media down to more junior associates or trainees.

This not only frees up your time, it is also a very practical personal development exercise for those you are delegating down to. It gets them involved in business development at a very early stage and will show them there is more to business development than just networking. It also requires them to research topics and come up with a cogent argument as to how the law can and should be applied in these situations, which will only help their development as lawyers.

4. Outsource

If there is absolutely no time or resource available, it may be worth enlisting the help of a specialist. Irrespective of where you are based and which area of law you practice, there will be a number of experienced and capable marketing professionals who would welcome the opportunity to manage your blog and article writing and your social media presence.

Admittedly, they will not be able to deliver your webinars or host your online events, but they will be able to organize them and create the marketing campaigns you'll need to promote them.

The final consideration is the one we looked at in the last chapter. If all of this is going to come together, you need to remain flexible. Be ready to adapt and improvise should the situation change which, without sounding pessimistic, it almost certainly will and probably without warning.

While I appreciate the analogy may be a little dated, think about a classic 1980s stack stereo. More specifically, think about the graphic equalizers that took up most of their front panels.

If you're too young to remember graphic equalizers, they were made up of a series of knobs and dials that allowed you to control the different frequency bands a stereophonic track is made up of, so you could adapt any piece of music to meet your preferences.

That system of knobs and dials is a good illustration of how you will need to control your business development plan.

Sometimes you will need to turn some things up and other things down, depending on what is allowed and what isn't. And, just as with a graphic equalizer, the settings will probably need to be tweaked from track to track or, in the case of your business development plan, from month to month if not week to week.

As restrictions are reduced you'll turn up the face-to-face elements while maintaining a steady level of content and social media presence. If restrictions tighten again, you will need to turn down the face-to-face level and increase online events, perhaps organising a video panel discussion or a virtual hospitality event.

Chapter 7: The perfect opportunity to refresh the way you do business

Whether you are speaking to clients on video or by phone, in person or via more formal client listening programs, you will be collecting a huge amount of up-to-the-minute insight into what your clients want from you and how they want to receive your services.

Managed correctly, these conversations will be capturing:

- Your clients' primary concerns;
- Their future plans;
- The changes they want to make to their business or personal affairs;
- Why they want to make these changes;
- What they need to implement these changes;
- How and where they plan to work from now on;
- What will work best in terms of how you will support those preferences moving forward;
- What they consider to be genuine added value; and
- How best to provide that added value.

All of this insight is invaluable.

It will tell you exactly what you need to do to ensure your firm remains current, relevant, and competitive within what is already a heavily disrupted legal market. It will signpost how you can make yourself the most attractive option as the market hardens and you have to fight harder for your share of what could be significantly less work. It will also give you the strongest possible marketing messages by defining added value and allowing you to bend your delivery to the specific demands of a client base who themselves are in flux.

However, it can only make the contribution to your future that it should if you use it. So my next question is, how will you use it?

Why do you need to act on this insight?

During the credit crunch of 2008, many firms said that the ensuing recession had to herald a period of massive change for the legal market. This, they said, was the clarion cry for wholesale changes including:

- The paperless office;
- The birth of greater fluidity between ranks to ensure maximum cost-efficiency for clients; and
- The death of both partner-heavy structures and the billable hour.

These changes never came, at least not in any meaningful way.

Many legal commentators have now been quick to go on record to say the current pandemic *will* finally force the legal profession to make these changes.

This means that the successful law firm of the near future is likely to look very different. Part of this will be because the demands of its clients will be very different. However, the ongoing changes to our traditional working practices and the predicted rethinking of our cities' historic business districts will also play their part. With that in mind, the process of adapting to those demands – in terms of your structure, offering and delivery – is not one you can afford to put off.

The good news is, as you are already gathering the insight you'll need to tell you what changes you need to make, you can take this opportunity to start identifying the next steps in your firm's development.

If you use this insight constructively you will be able to:

- Position your firm as dynamic, forward-thinking, and innovative;
- Operate more effectively (and more profitably) within the new trading environment;
- Meet the new demands of your clients more immediately;
- Stand out from your competitors in what will be a much harder legal market; and
- Retain and develop the staff you know are capable of helping you achieve the growth you want.

While this book is written from a business development perspective, my suggestion is you need to define business development as more than just sales and marketing. Instead, think of it as the means to develop your business so you are ready for whatever the new legal market looks like. Ask yourself what you need to do in order to:

- Meet your clients' changing (legal and professional) needs;
- Build a team capable of meeting these demands in what will be a very new trading environment for all of us; and
- Make savings and improve your processes to maximize efficiencies and protect your cash position.

Then review your thinking by comparing it with the data you gain from both your own client development activities and any more formal client listening programs. What you need to do will be in the common themes.

During this process, you will end up having to consider more than just the way you look after your clients and contacts and the way you promote yourself within your chosen market/s. If used correctly, your findings will potentially impact on every part of your business plan so you can develop the best way to articulate, promote, sell, do, deliver, and bill for your services in a single and seamless action.

The four pillars of a successful organization

In terms of the different parts of your business plan, a successful business tends to be built around four pillars – people, promotion, finance, and systems.

People

Does your team have the requisite experience (in terms of years served and of the specific sector or market understanding your clients need)?

Are you balanced in terms of partners versus associates and paralegals so you can do your work at the right levels to ensure profitability and quality?

With regards to anyone who has been lost either permanently or temporarily during the pandemic, have you worked out which need to be replaced and which you can manage without? Or if increasing your headcount isn't currently an option, have you worked out which of your staff would be best to focus on in terms of fast-tracking them into the positions you need to fill?

Promotion

This is basically the sales and marketing function we have already explored in detail.

Are you effective in the way you educate your clients about all of the services you provide? Do you have a well-articulated and well-distributed set of sales messages? Are those messages permeating the right markets and are your various activities yielding the desired results?

From a more commercial perspective, which activities can you lose and which do you need to do more of to positively impact your bottom line?

Are you using your clients' opinions to make more informed marketing decisions? For example, are you acting on their advice when they tell you about the events, groups, publications, websites etc. they are telling you have real traction and influence within their market/s?

Finance

Obviously, you won't be discussing the ins and outs of your balance sheet or the individual financial performance of certain lawyers with anyone outside the firm, but you should be talking about the financial factors they see.

For example, you could ask about the efficacy and accuracy of your fee estimates, your clients' appetite for alternative billing structures, the transparency of your invoices and how they feel your fees compare to their expectations and/or the other professional advisers they use.

Systems

I cannot even begin to pretend I understand a law firm's IT infrastructure or the machinations of the back office, but this is what "systems" covers. It is an area where even the smallest improvements can make huge incremental differences to your performance and your profitability.

While we have been working remotely we have picked up a lot of good habits in terms of the way we use tech to communicate and the way we have reduced reliance on print and paper. We've even finally managed to lose some of the more archaic administrative processes we got used to while we were all in the same office. But can we do more?

How do your clients think your workflow processes could be streamlined and what packages could help you realize that faster, leaner, and more client-efficient shape?

The good news is all the requisite technology is already available.

Deep down, we already knew this. The legal press is awash with advertisements and advertorials promoting the next big thing. The real issue is how we use it to benefit the firm. How can our tech be updated and refined so it actually improves the way fee earners interact with technology every day and improves the way we engage with our clients?

Again, their steer as to what they want will help bring that part of the puzzle into much sharper focus before you make any decisions as to which changes you need to make.

As technology really isn't my thing, I spoke to Alex Hutchinson of the Chatham Group who specializes in helping law firms progress IT, software, case management, and technology projects. I asked Alex if he could add a little more insight and maybe provide some simple points for you to bear in mind. Below is his advice:

> *"Technology should help law firms improve the way their fee earners deliver work for their clients. At the same time, it should also improve the way your clients interact and communicate with you, whether that is when you are opening a new file, reporting progress, or simply keeping in touch. IT should be there to make life easier, not harder or more frustrating, which still happens far too often.*
>
> *"A lot of the time, law firms select technology via a laborious tender process, implement it and expect it to work. The problem is it doesn't. This is because the implementation hasn't been managed correctly and/or the supporting training is minimal and generic. It suddenly becomes apparent that using the kit in real life is not how it looked during the sales demonstration.*
>
> *"This isn't solely down to the provider. The key to successfully adopting new technology is to start the process by looking at how you can (and want) to deliver a better service to your clients – which the clients will tell you during your conversations with them – and how you can improve the working lives and efficiency of your fee earners.*
>
> *"The biggest mistake we see is firms look to suppliers for solutions and answers. You need to remember they are there to sell you something so already have their own answers! Instead, you should start by clearly defining what you need, how you would like it to work, and why.*
>
> *"Where do you find this information? Well, that's easy. Again, it's about speaking to your clients and your fee earners to see what they need to improve their lives, and the answers to these questions have to come from your clients and your colleagues, not from salespeople. Once you have their answers you can go and find the right solutions."*

Your conversations with your clients and contacts should touch on all four of these pillars in some way or at least invite feedback that will help you update and refresh each area.

Chapter 8:
Refreshing the four pillars of your firm

As things are still so fluid, your number one priority has, of course, to be to do the things that will keep more work coming in over the short-term.

However, as I said at the start of the last chapter, your market will be looking for a different type of law firm once we get through this pandemic; the world will have changed and your clients' needs, preferences, and expectations will change with it.

While change is probably the last thing you want to think about with so much else to worry about, I'd urge you not to put it off. You really will need to take a slightly different approach and you need to start considering what that approach will have to look like now if you are going to be ready to fully capitalise on the next stage of your market's development.

I also want to be very clear that I'm not talking about the type of legal services you provide per se; these won't change. People will still need to buy houses, write and execute wills, and get divorced. Businesses will still need employment advice, property leases, commercial contracts, IP rights and M&A support.

What I'm talking about is making the necessary changes to maintain a healthy, relevant, and profitable practice. For example:

- What do you need to adapt in the way you deliver your services?
- What will be the best way to take care of your clients?
- What will you need to do to promote your firm and attract new clients?
- What can technology do to make you more efficient and more accessible?
- What fat can you trim so you do not have to cover unnecessary costs?

Similarly, I'm not talking about throwing the baby out with the bathwater. Your clients like your firm; they have been loyal to your firm.

This means the constituent elements of your offering should again largely stay the same.

However, solid foundations for the future need to be laid. You need to start to put everything in place so you can move gradually towards where you know you should be – where your clients and contacts have *told* you that you should be – over the coming months.

The feedback you have received will complement your own reading of the market. You should use a combination of both to table the questions you'll need to answer in the internal discussions you hold about the future of your firm.

Obviously, the nature of your discussions will depend on the practice areas you offer, your commercial objectives, your target markets (current and aspirational), your location, your resources, your budget and, perhaps most crucially, the feedback you've received.

However, to give you an idea of some of the types of areas we have been helping our clients to refresh over the past few months, I thought it may be useful to share some examples here.

People

Do you have the right people?

From a practical point of view this means having enough bodies to manage the work in ratio to the volume of work each area brings in. If you have some areas that are over-staffed for the level of work they generate, then it may be time to make some difficult decision so these practice areas can go back to making the contribution they should.

On the other hand, if you are stretched too thin in other areas then maybe recruitment should become a priority. The last thing you want is for clients to suffer a drop in service levels as that could unsettle their faith in the firm.

The other way to look at your team is from an attitudinal point of view. As the trading environment becomes tougher, you need to know you can count on all of your fee earners. You want drive, energy, and ideas, not shrinking violets. You want people who are willing to push themselves forward – regardless of their personal motivations – and do what is needed to keep the firm in the healthiest possible state.

I hate to say it in print, but if you have serious doubts over any members of your team, this may be the time to go your separate ways. This is not a time for tolerating passengers.

And just because I'm a BD guy, please don't think I am only promoting the retention of your keenest business developers. As we go through some of these examples you'll see there is as much work to do in the back office with your finances, systems, and the development of your people. Most of all, you need to know you will have enough of the right people to keep the work moving whilst continuing to deliver the highest levels of quality and service.

Are your people at the right levels to do the work profitably?

Sometimes when a firm is hit by unforeseen economic factors it is the junior members of staff who feel the brunt of any changes. This is totally understandable. As a partnership you want to protect your partners and it is often easier to lose the people you aren't as close to.

However, from a purely commercial perspective, is this the right thing to do?

If you do have to make changes to your team, those changes need to take into account how things will work after the changes have been made and why you are looking to make the changes in the first place.

Often the most profitable law firms – and I stress there are huge exceptions depending on the type of work and type of lawyers involved – are the ones that operate in the triangular model; a few partners at the top, a few more senior associates under them, then a wider base of junior lawyers supporting them.

This model allows work to be dealt with at the appropriate level rather than forcing lower level work up and into the hands of a more expensive partner. Better still, managing work in this way offers the client greater cost efficiency and usually facilitates a faster turnaround.

Before you make any decisions, take the time to make an honest assessment of what you have and what type of model works best for both your clients and your bottom line. One phrase I am hearing more and more recently is:

"Don't sacrifice your long-term goals for short-term savings."

For me, this is excellent advice and well worth taking.

Do you have the required succession, retention, and personal development plans in place?

Whatever changes you make to your staff, you cannot afford to let cracks appear in your teams or your service delivery.

If you have lost any senior people, do you have a worthy replacement ready to step into their shoes? When a client relationship has been a close one for a number of years, the time just before and just after the lead partner leaves is when the firm's relationship is at greatest risk.

This means the new point of contact has to be prepared to overinvest in the relationship and, given they probably can't go out and see the client, this needs to be done by using the tactics we've discussed earlier the book.

With that in mind, if you are planning to bid farewell to a colleague it is never too soon to begin the succession process. As soon as you know someone will be leaving the firm, make sure you have nominated a successor (better still, find reasons to introduce a couple of possibilities so your client can make their own choice) and begin the transition. If you leave this too late the client could well feel neglected.

Likewise, have you identified the partners of tomorrow? If you have then they need to be mentored and receive the training they'll need to run your business – in areas such as client development, business development, HR, and finance. They also need to be enthused and more closely involved in your plans (particularly in terms of knowing the part you want them to play in your firm's future).

It is just an observation, but some firms I have worked with have lost some of their potential stars simply because they didn't know the bright future their partner had planned for them. This left large (and expensive) holes to fill and was totally avoidable.

Do you need to revise your remuneration, rewards and incentives?

People are any firm's main expenditure by some distance. While annual bonuses are of course an almost ubiquitous benefit within the legal sector today, the salary (or dividend, profit share, or PEP if you are a partner) plus bonus model is not the only option. Nor do you have to adopt a one-size-fits-all approach.

As cash will be more stretched for the coming months, this could be the time to look at alternative remuneration options. The one thing you will want to avoid at all costs is cutting hours (unless that is what a particular lawyer has asked to do for work/life reasons) and cutting pay accordingly. But could you reduce salaries and introduce more attractive incentive payments if certain performance criteria are met?

These criteria can of course include, but should never be limited to, billing totals. Staff also need to remain aware they will be rewarded for their contribution to helping the firm successfully navigate the next few months. Depending on the area each lawyer would like to assist with, your targets could include things like marketing and business development, assistance with practice management, mentoring and developing colleagues, and the implementation of new technology.

For partners who take a full share but are unwilling to do what is required to grow or even more actively manage their client base, consultancy deals linked directly to financial performance could be considered. Alternatively, these lawyers might prefer to take a fixed share, which would leave more to be divided by fewer "true" partners (i.e. those motivated to increase fees and profits) at the end of the year.

These measures needn't be limited to fee earners either. Support staff can also be incentivised beyond their duties. Introducing work is easy to measure, manage, and reward, but additional criteria like new ideas, mentoring, and assuming increased responsibility can also be considered.

A note of caution. Because of the crucial part our pay plays in our lives, this is – bar redundancy – the most emotive subject in any workplace. This means that any change has to be made following a detailed consultation with all of the affected members of staff, and the potential upside has to exceed what is currently being offered.

Promotion

We have already covered identifying, strengthening, and leveraging your key relationships and the tactics required to open up and capitalise on potential new markets.

However, the one area of your promotion that your feedback could identify that needs to be adapted is your offering, or to give it its full marketing name, your client value proposition.

Your clients look at the firm purely from an external market perspective, regardless of whether they are a business or an individual. This means they can see things that you, even with the best of intentions, can't from within the firm. While you are having your conversations with clients and contacts, try to eke out what they think about:

- Why they work with you;
- What you do well;
- What you don't do (well or otherwise);
- What you need to do differently;
- Where you add real value;
- How well they think you articulate and promote your message;

- Whether they feel your marketing reflects the firm/people that they work with;
- Where they believe you sit within your particular part of the legal market; and
- How they think you rank against your competitors.

Once you have this insight you can start to discuss whether you need to update the messaging on your website and your marketing material and what you convey when you are talking to your clients.

This is important for two reasons. Firstly, what could have been a strong and credible message before the pandemic may not be quite as relevant today, so if changes are required to help you maintain your competitive advantage, you should make them now.

Secondly, people (and this applies perhaps more to prospective clients, although some existing clients may also be considering going back out to tender) are making more decisions based on internet research and formal procurement. Your ability to win new work, therefore, is more dependent on the way you articulate your value proposition than it ever has been before.

Finance

How does your pricing benchmark against your closest competitors?

Although clients' sensitivity to price has grown steadily since 2008, the current situation has heightened it further still. This means that if your fees are markedly higher than your competitors you could be missing out on new opportunities and even be at risk of your clients moving to another firm.

Conversely, if your fees are much lower than your competitors, you could maybe look to increase them slightly. This will have an immediate impact on your bottom line and could alleviate a little of the short-term pressure on your cashflow.

There are of course instances when a straight cost comparison is a fair means of measurement.

If you possess genuine specialisms – in terms of specific types of work or specific types of clients – you can charge a premium. As a recognised expert, your clients will accept this has to be the case. This is because what you can do for them will deliver a great deal more benefit and value than the client would receive from a cheaper option that can't offer the same depth of understanding or the same ability to apply the law to the very particular nuances of their world.

How well does your physical billing process suit your clients?

Historically, a law firm's billing process was designed to suit the firm. Then once it was in place, it was only revisited in extreme circumstances (i.e. when a client specifically said they'd like it done a different way).

However, because of the additional pressures and concerns clients are facing due to the current situation, this may be time to make your billing processes more client-friendly. Have you ever taken the time to ask your clients what their preferred frequency, timing, and format would be?

Many companies now prefer to be invoiced electronically, especially from an environmental perspective. If this is something you have not yet put in place it may be worth doing so. Not only does it save paper, it also saves time (email arrives immediately) and if you also add a single-click payment mechanism, the speed at which you are paid could also increase.

Similarly, falling in line with your clients' payment cycles will also benefit your cash collection. Try and find out how often and/or on which days of the month they execute their BACS transfers and make sure your bills arrive several days before.

Finally, have you ever asked your clients how they would like the invoice to be populated? This is another gripe we hear during client interviews. Sometimes because of the time lags between work being requested, work being done, and work being billed, the client has no way of telling exactly what is covered in each invoice. This can end up causing the client time as they have to get in touch with you or your billing department to find what it covers out for themselves. Not only does this cause annoyance but it can also slow the payment process, which again will impact on your cashflow.

How well does your billing process suit your colleagues?

I may be entering dangerous waters here, but I think we all know some lawyers bill better than others!

Some are happy to send a regular bill (which is better for cash flow) but others save up their bills to send all at once at the conclusion of a matter. This is fine if you work in a transactional area, for example if you are writing a will or preparing a one-off contract or lease. But if you work on longer-term matters, billing in this way will not only slow your cash flow, it could put you at risk of the client being so staggered by the number at the bottom of the invoice that they question the bill and you have to write off part of the total.

Estimates are another contentious area. Some estimate low to win the work then wonder why clients are annoyed that the final fee is significantly higher than they anticipated. Some don't flag when extra work will lead to extra cost and are then faced with irate clients questioning bills. This too can lead to having to write off part of the bill and, as the subsequent discussions will all take time to resolve, will also have an effect on your cashflow.

These may seem like trivial points but I can assure you that during the client interviews I've been involved in, "nasty surprises" are still one of the most regular complaints.

Clients don't appreciate bills they weren't expecting and it can lead to unrest. Given the nervousness in all quarters at the moment, this could cost you clients.

Meanwhile, once you have made your decisions you will need to set uniform pricing, estimate and billing protocols internally to balance your clients' demands with the best financial interests of your firm. You'll then need to police them to make sure they are being followed.

I know that the majority of partnerships still prefer to maintain a very collegiate feel but this is not always the most commercial approach. Just as you need to ensure there is clear accountability for client development and new client acquisition, your lawyers also need to be personally accountable for their billing and credit control (albeit with the support of the relevant members of your support staff). If the protocols you set are not being adhered to by some colleagues, there needs to be consequence. If you face any reticence, remind those colleagues that as fee levels are likely to drop in the short-term while the recession rights itself, the fees you do bill have to be managed and collected in the most effective manner to protect the firm.

Do you need to explore alternative billing processes?

The crash in 2008 was supposed to put the final nail into the billable hour model. While this didn't actually happen, it has made many firms reappraise the way that they charge, and fixed fees, risk/reward and hybrid billing models have increased in popularity (particularly, it has to be said, with clients).

With cash likely to be more scarce and more carefully appropriated, this is definitely the time to start to look at how you could make more of your billing processes (and by "more" I mean strengthen your client relationships while making yourself look more forward-thinking and therefore attractive to prospective new clients during the pitch or tender process).

Fixed fees are the most obvious choice. Clients like fixed fees because they offer cost certainty. For many, the billable hour process is too open-ended – if there have been multiple instances of your firm coming in above your initial estimates, that could be sowing unhelpful seeds of doubt in your clients' minds. You don't need me to tell you that doubt is definitely not something you want to engender with so much uncertainty around at the moment.

Generally, the reason lawyers are nervous about offering fixed fees is they feel they will end up recovering less time than they've spent. In some instances this will happen. In others, the work will take less time than expected so the highly unscientific rule of swings and roundabouts should kick in by the end of your financial year.

If you are still unconvinced, perhaps you could adopt a halfway house to get you started. For litigation of family practices this could involve a fixed fee to a certain point (i.e. making your initial approaches). After that you'd have to return to an hourly model or submit a cost for the next block of work as your involvement will of course depend on the initial response you receive from the other side.

Or you could limit fixed fees to the most transactional pieces of work you do (e.g. preparing a contract of employment, drafting a shareholder's agreement, clearing and filing a trademark or writing a will). You should know from experience how long this takes so setting a fee that will work in the majority of cases should be achievable.

Capped fees is something else clients like. It allows you to maintain some degree of flexibility but also gives your client the reassurance your total fee will not exceed a certain level and the feeling you are looking out for them.

Risk/reward is definitely the most risky option but does also offer the highest potential reward. With clients facing their own trials and tribulations, if the risk and reward can be balanced (at least theoretically) the PR halo of even offering that type of arrangement could be huge even if it's not actually accepted.

Personally, I would stick to fixed and capped fees until the trading environment has settled down and become slightly more predictable.

What is your plan for your fixed assets?

Aside from your staff, the highest costs you need to cover are probably your premises. Given that in all likelihood we will all end up working partly from home and partly in the office, do you still need the total square footage you had at the start of the pandemic?

Our city centres have become a shadow of what they were. Many people opted to work from home even when their offices opened. Studies suggest this trend will only continue when things do finally get back to "normal". It has been widely reported that almost 70 percent of lawyers have said they now want to work at home, not only for reasons of health and safety but also because of the greater flexibility it affords their personal life.

This has led to property experts predicting a very different future for our city centres as large-scale offices are downsized and interiors remodelled to accommodate more hot desking and "hoteling" options, as well as more socially distanced meeting facilities. There is also talk of adapting the extra room this will leave to provide a higher level of staff benefits, such as subsidised gyms and onsite catering.

This is the time to consider what you need in terms of real estate moving forward. Can you afford to downsize? Do you need to remodel your interiors to meet the new working arrangements of your fee earners and/or improve your client experience?

Also, do you need your smaller branch offices? This is immaterial to a large commercially focused firm with a widespread clientbase but it has been a very hot topic for more regionally focused clients.

On the one hand, this is absolutely the time to maintain a local presence to show clients you are committed to their communities and are available and accessible should they need you. On the other, with your lawyers working from home, can you not reposition their home offices as a network of even more branch offices?

While this is unashamedly marketing spin, it is true. You can lose the cost of your additional offices but still have people on the doorstep as and when they're needed. With the increasing number of serviced office options, you could maintain an attractive meeting space should you need one.

If you own your building, could sub-letting be an option? If you are a tenant, it may be worth renegotiating your lease or even looking for a break so you can – over time – find new premises that meet your requirements.

And if you are to move, maybe you could consider an out-of-town location if city centres are no longer the attractive destination for clients they once were.

Systems

Technology has a massive role to play if you are going to get your people, promotion, and finances right. Without even straying into the maelstrom that is AI, even the simplest "off-the-shelf" legal tech can help you become faster, leaner, and more efficient in a number of areas. Depending on the improvements that your clients have told you they want to see, my advice would be to work out exactly what you want to achieve then work backwards to identify the best option to pursue.

Although I would always suggest you work through this process with an independent expert (as Alex of The Chatham Group said in the previous chapter, independence is always preferable to working with a representative who will prioritise their own product range), the following questions may be helpful in terms of getting your conversations moving and forming some initial discussions:

- Do you have the technology required to support the changes you want to make in terms of the way you deliver your services?
- Do you have the technology required to provide your clients with the access and transparency they want?
- Do you have the technology required to support deals while your team and your clients are all working from multiple locations?
- Do you have the technology you'll need to support the changes you want to make to your back office?
- Do you have the technology you'll need to communicate effectively internally, externally and across multiple locations?
- Do you have the technology required to facilitate the virtual business development activities you will have to implement?

Chapter 9: Practical planning – how to create an effective 90-day plan

As things start to become more settled, it's time to look slightly further ahead. Move to planning in 90-day blocks and, where possible, introduce more involved "campaign" style activities rather than delivering a series of single-action initiatives.

This will allow you to spread your personal or team focus to include all of the potential sources of new work – existing clients, professional contacts, and new business – whilst maintaining some higher degree of flexibility in case restrictions change again and you are forced to re-evaluate what you can and can't achieve.

The template below is designed to help you plan your BD activities on a quarterly basis and keep those activities on one page so that you have a single but simple point of reference that is easy to follow and easy to update if required.

As well as remaining mindful that your plan should cover clients, contacts, and targets, it is also worth remembering that tactically you need to continue to mix virtual activities with physical ones. You also need to stay attuned to the fact that as we work our way through the quarters of the next year, the ratio by which you balance the virtual with the physical will naturally change.

As with the 30-day plan that was included in part one of this book, your business development will always be more productive when you (and your colleagues if you are taking more of a team approach) are matching activities they are best suited to. Have a look at the plan on the next page.

To give you a better idea, on the page after that there is a working example of how a completed plan could look.

Name:
Period:

Project	Tasks	Actions	Date of delivery	Action owner	Status

Figure 6: The 90-day plan template.

Name:
Period:

Project	Tasks	Actions	Date of delivery	Action owner	Status
Increase individual client contribution	Create development plans for our top 20 percent Implement the required tactics to grow annual spend Launch a virtual events calendar	Deliver agreed actions for Q1	End of 12/20		Complete
		Review next steps in departmental meetings	Every meeting		Ongoing
		Review financials	Every meeting		Ongoing
		Sign off calendar	End of 12/20		Complete
		Run Q1 events	End of 01/21		TBC
Increase our lawyers' individual contribution to business development	Complete/launch personal BD plans Provide BD coaching to support the plans All lawyers to exceed targets and hit associated KPIs	Sign off plans	End of 11/20		Complete
		Lawyers to implement individual action plans	Next actions delivered monthly		Ongoing
		Deliver group training	11/20-02/21		Launched/ongoing
		Set up coaching program	11/20-02/21		Launched/ongoing
		Review progress on BD actions/financials	Monthly one-on-one		Ongoing
Increase operational efficiency	Implement new electronic payment system Reduce aged debt	Transfer to new system	01/01/21		TBC
		Deliver training	End of 01/21		TBC
		Produce month-by-month comparison	Monthly		Ongoing
		Partners discuss underperformance with lawyers	As required		Ongoing

Figure 7: An example of a 90-day plan.

Part 3:
Return

Chapter 10: What do we know about the future?

To borrow a phrase to make a point, we are not about to go back to the future. At least, we're not going back to a future any of us can predict.

The last few months have seen us undergo – often without really knowing it – an absolutely seismic shift in the way we live. Within this unmitigated period of change, consumer behavior has been one of the things that has altered most.

If we use some examples from our everyday lives rather than our professional lives, we have seen even the most straightforward businesses completely refresh the way they go to market and the way they service their customers. Local restaurants introduced home delivery services and the ability to "click and collect"; fitness instructors started to use Zoom to host their classes; and retailers of all shapes and sizes expanded their online offerings.

Even our schools (operations that haven't really had to update themselves in any way for centuries) were at the vanguard of change. They quickly moved lessons from the classroom onto laptops so they could continue to give their "customers" what they needed from the safety of their homes.

Strangely, it was supermarkets – a sector that had actually been at the forefront of online ordering for home delivery – that struggled. They hadn't appreciated the spike in demand for their services and, therefore, hadn't prepared adequately. As a result, consumer confidence was shaken and their failures allowed smaller, local grocers to jump in and introduce better, more reliable services.

But while all of these stories are already familiar, what do the underlying trends mean for the legal industry? For me, the key trend to pay attention to is that COVID-19 has finally proved we no longer *go* online, we *live* online.

This shift is arguably one that's been in progress for the last 15 years. However, the fact we could no longer make the choice between real and online life has increased the speed of transfer to a rate that none of us would have predicted on New Year's Eve 2019.

The result is this transfer from real to online life has forced us to become not only virtual lawyers but, in many aspects of our life, virtual people.

In simple terms this means that if you are going to return your firm to where it was – whether that return is judged by revenue, profitability, market share, or size – you will have to come to terms with exactly how the virus has changed the way we buy, sell, and communicate. These are the lessons that will inform a successful business development plan moving forward.

All of the following is based purely on my opinion. I am neither clairvoyant nor am I privy to more than what I've seen, read, and witnessed since March. I do, however, feel strongly that what I have seen, read, and witnessed is starting to form a reasonably clear picture of the trends we will need to follow to ensure our future success.

Buy, sell, and communicate – externally

We will be increasingly home-based

Studies across a multitude of professions and cross-sections of the population offer irrefutable proof that our working lives will be very different when this all ends. Depending on which study you read, the number of people who are able to work from home who would prefer to work from home for the majority of the working week is regularly over 70 percent.

This means that a successful commercial future now depends on being able to match those preferences and provide easy and effective ways to communicate with and deliver services to clients, irrespective of where they (and we) are at any given time.

It also means that clients or customers will be less likely to travel to providers to purchase the products and services they want, regardless of how high their desire for those products and services is.

I read a staggering statistic the other day. Apparently the number of miles that will be driven by US citizens will have decreased by 270 billion this year. While that figure will of course rise once the current situation changes, if the majority of people who have reduced their mileage so drastically haven't seen their ability to do what they need to suffer, or have found out they actually prefer the alternative, I cannot see the number returning to former levels any time soon.

Home-working is not simply about location. Since we have been working at home the working day has become a much more flexible concept. Some people now prefer to start earlier to finish earlier or start later to finish later. Some take a few hours off in the middle of the day to cover childcare or simply to give them a bit of a break to exercise in. Some are working shorter weekdays and making the time back over the weekend.

Others have even adopted an "as and when approach", which makes it even harder for marketers to reach them, let alone catch their attention.

Given we are not all working the same hours or even days, the question of what a business needs to do to make sure they reach the highest possible percentage of their market with every interaction has never been so difficult to answer.

What can be done online will be done online

We've already looked at the enormous impact the ability to market and sell online has had on retail (a 97 percent increase between May and July 2020 for Walmart alone), hospitality, and education, but the opportunities offered by the internet have now spread far wider than that. It now appears there is a way to do everything online.

Who would have thought we'd be having virtual family parties? Or that the biggest occasions in our lives – our weddings, birthdays, and new additions to our families – would be celebrated online?

From a legal perspective – or at least the UK legal perspective – many of the core activities we thought could only be done in person are now moving online. We are seeing more and more online court hearings, online arbitrations involving protagonists in as many locations as there are people involved, and new legislation has even been passed to allow wills and other legal documents to be witnessed via Zoom.

I am old enough to remember when many people were nervous about internet banking. Those days are well and truly gone. It seems that necessity has made us accept that if it can be done online, it's OK to do it online.

A greater thirst for knowledge

Whether it's a result of social distancing making us more willing to search out the solutions and background information we need, or just because we have more time on our hands whilst working remotely, the fact is the number of searches is growing so fast that no meaningful statistics can be produced.

At the start of the pandemic many of these searches were unsurprisingly very specific and linked to finding out the most pertinent details relating to something none of us had ever come across before:

- What is coronavirus?
- How do I make a mask?
- How contagious is coronavirus?
- Can children pass on coronavirus?
- How do you make hand sanitizer?

Then, once the initial rush for information was over, the searches started to become more practical, focusing in on how to make the best of a bad situation:

- How do I set up a home office?
- What is the best internet connection for a home office?
- How do you conference call?
- How to do you use MS Teams?
- How do I mute myself on Zoom?

At the same time, spikes started to appear that hinted we needed to keep ourselves going as much as our businesses. Search terms like "yoga", "mental wellbeing apps", "home gym", "online gym", "resistance bands bikes", "learn a language" and "best hobbies for lockdown" all started to gather momentum.

While this is an interesting sociological snapshot, it is also a hugely invaluable prompt for law firms. What this signals is people want more information and they are prepared to spend time online finding it. These are habits that are now fully imbedded and will be sustained even once restrictions are fully lifted.

But we are not only gathering the information we need online. The media also has a part to play. According to statistics released in September 2020, 61 percent of interviewees said they planned to continue to watch more news after the outbreak. This trend is reflected in app downloads, which show a steep rise in demand for apps that provide rolling news, healthcare, and educational content.

The DIY boom

With certain "non-essential" businesses (a questionable phrase as I doubt the owners of those businesses see themselves as anything less than essential for their clients/customers) being forced to close during certain periods, we have all had to turn our hands to all sorts of things, including haircuts, repairs, and baking.

By extension, the demand for "how to" guides and the products required to do all of these things has grown. If you look at the traffic going through the relevant discussion forums, that too has grown.

DIY is arguably the most likely trend to drop once all of the services we need have reopened and it is arguably the least relevant to the professional services market but it is an acknowledged trend which is why I mention it here.

Buy, sell, and communicate – internally

The rise of technology

Every law firm had to adapt quickly to the demands of working virtually. Using more technology and in ever increasingly sophisticated ways has been key to this transformation. One only has to look at the speed at which our existing platforms have continued to develop and the speed at which new alternatives have hit the market to see that this is not a temporary fad. Technology will definitely have a huge part to play as the demands and structure of the new legal market becomes clearer and its influence will stretch across all four pillars of your firm:

1. It will continue to make your people more effective in terms of the way they manage their workflow and continue to improve the way you communicate both internally and externally.
2. It will continue to allow you to improve the way you take your message to market, whether that is for client development or new client acquisition purposes. It will also continue to provide new and ever more productive and cost-effective ways to communicate so you achieve and maintain the market position you want.
3. It will allow you to manage your finances more efficiently, both in terms of improving reporting processes and the way you bill and collect cash.
4. It will allow you to optimize your day-to-day operations and cut out any unnecessary, labor-intensive, and expensive processes, which in turn will impact positively on your profitability.

While there will be a cost implication of keeping up with the latest technology it is not unfortunately a cost that can be cut if you genuinely want your firm to remain relevant, credible, and capable of meeting the next demands of your clients. The good news, however, is that it is a cost that will generate a tangible return, as choosing the right tech will increase both your efficiency and your profitability.

Keeping clients engaged

As the crisis hit us all at the same time and forced us all to make the same changes to the way we worked and lived – most notably moving meeting in person to meeting over video – the move to a virtual working environment has largely been successful.

While there is no doubt that video meetings are here to stay, there will always be a need for physical meetings. Yes, video is arguably more efficient (no travel, negligible cost, the time you meet is only the time you meet) but a real lawyer/client relationship is about much more than just being able to talk. It's about establishing a personal connection, trust, and just being comfortable in each other's company.

This means that it is essential firms establish a hybrid that takes full advantage of the efficiencies offered by virtual BD and the ability to progress the personal side offered by physical BD.

However, there is also your clients' (and prospective clients') engagement with the firm to consider. How will you create communications campaigns that will really engage your audience?

Pursuing new opportunities

The process of winning new work will always be driven by your ability to engage clients and prospects, but the ability to identify and pursue new opportunities also has a large part to play.

As the legal market starts to stabilize, "relevance" and "situation" will quickly become one of the most important themes in marketing and business development.

- Can you provide relevant advice for the specific situations your clients and targets are currently facing?
- Is your messaging relevant to the situations your clients and contacts face?
- Are you making yourself the most relevant choice by putting yourself in your clients' and contacts' current situation?

It is probably the most frequently recurring theme in this book, but all of the answers will come from sticking close to your clients and contacts.

They are the best possible source of insight as to what is relevant and what their situation is. Once you have that insight you can start to spot new opportunities across your market, including:

- Cross-selling opportunities;
- New "products" (how can you package the advice you provide in more client-friendly ways and what other services do you need to introduce through lateral hires or collaborations?);
- New introductions;
- Ideas on how to improve your service offering;
- Potential marketing platforms; and
- Finding out what is about to happen in your market so you can prepare accordingly.

We have all been through a lot since March 2020, and taken huge strides forward in terms of mitigating what could have been a disaster for the legal profession. The future depends on our ability to keep spotting (and acting on) new opportunities.

Traditionally the legal market has been somewhat unfairly viewed as slow moving and risk-averse but the speed at which law firms adapted to the pandemic has done a lot to dispel that. However, that momentum will be lost if you do not capitalize on it and continue to do everything you can to identify and pursue new opportunities.

Returning to the office

Despite setback after setback and the majority of lawyers' reported desire to continue to work from home, at some point there will be some sort of return to the office .

There have already been wide ranging discussion in most firms as to what this will look like. These discussions will almost certainly have also involved consideration of the type/size of office that will be needed going forward and whether a reduction or repurposing of your firm's current square footage is required.

We have looked at some of these factors in an earlier chapter so perhaps it is worth looking at the argument for having an office environment.

While some lawyers have definitely enjoyed working from home because of the extra time and head space it provides and the level of distraction it has taken away, for most of us there is a much needed social aspect that only a shared working environment can provide.

Mental health has quite rightly been a heavily debated topic recently, particularly while we have had to work remotely and individually. A return to the office – whether that is managed in shifts, teams, by hot desking, or any other type of rota to maintain social distancing – will address the potential for isolation and allow us to continue to have much needed social interaction with our colleagues and, eventually, our clients and contacts.

Aside from the mental health aspects, your firm also has its culture to consider.

It is extremely difficult to maintain a set of common values and common practices if you do not share a common location. As was mentioned in an earlier chapter, good marketing requires consistency and even with the best of intentions and constant reminders, training, and cheerleading, consistency will dip unless there is also consistency of contact with colleagues and clients.

Aside from the social aspect there is also the development of your lawyers to consider.

Lawyers have always learned by "shadowing" more experienced colleagues. If your new recruits aren't in the same office, how effective will shadowing be?

Even if junior lawyers are invited into virtual meetings with clients, they won't have the same opportunity to observe the subtleties of the meeting that only interaction and body language can teach. In addition, from a purely business development perspective, simply logging on to a video call does not provide the type of "exam conditions" they'll need to practice small talk and the other crucial soft skills they'll depend on as their careers progress.

Supervision can be provided virtually but again, is it enough? Nothing can substitute the teacher/pupil dynamic of sitting side-by-side while a piece of work is reviewed. Sometimes marking via video can amplify the "criticism" rather than the "constructive" element of constructive criticism.

Even day-to-day management of more senior lawyers becomes more difficult when we're not seeing each other face-to-face. Many of the lawyers I have been working with since March have said there was originally a real drive to host team meetings (both work-focused and social) to keep their various teams together but the frequency has dipped or even disappeared now that video calls have become so commonplace and "Zoom fatigue" has taken hold.

This means that if we are going to continue to work from home, partners with management responsibility and heads of department are going to need to find new ways to keep their teams together, keep them communicating, and keep them motivated.

The return to the office isn't just about your current members of staff. Having a solid base will also help your future employees.

Integrating new joiners will be extremely challenging if it has to be done virtually. Some HR departments have worked hard to find alternative ways to onboard new lawyers, involving video links and distance learning style induction packages, but will those lawyers ever truly feel part of the firm without actually feeling the fabric of your firm every day?

When it comes to returning to the office, perhaps the last point to consider is the location of your office. Given we have found ways to successfully work remotely, does this augment the argument for "nearshoring"?

By relocating to less fashionable (and less expensive) areas you could save a considerable amount of rent. In addition, if you move to areas where local law firms have been hit hard, will there be a seam of talent you could mine to your immediate financial benefit? Or would your new location simply provide a cheaper base in which to house your support functions while your fee earners continue to work from home, popping into a smaller city center office when required?

New world, new threats

The downside of moving so much of a firm's operations online is that there is a much higher risk of becoming a victim of cybercrime. This risk is raised even higher when you consider so many fee earners are working from home in a less secure environment than they would be if they were on-site. This is not an area directly linked to business development, but it does have to be addressed. The negative feeling and publicity a cyberattack could garner would be hugely detrimental to all of your client development and new client acquisition efforts. It could also set your firm's reputation back immeasurably during what will already be a difficult time.

Keep moving forward

While we've looked at a number of ways for a law firm to assess and refresh their strategy to respond to the new ways of working that clients now want, success won't come from one round of changes. This has to be an ongoing process as things will continue to change while we all find our feet in whatever normal comes to mean.

But to end on a positive note, we have got this far and there have been no situations for which we haven't found at least a temporary solution. This frontier spirit will be vital to the next chapter of your firm's development. There really are no laurels to rest on at the moment; we need to keep things moving forward.

Chapter 11: How can we prepare our return to the future?

Although we don't know exactly how the future is going to look yet, we do know what we're going to have to work with in terms of putting a plan together to make sure your revenue, client base, and market position return to where they were before COVID-19.

External preferences	Internal considerations	Planning objectives
To work from home (or between home and office)	Make the best use of technology	To define how we will work (including managing the return to the office)
To do as much as possible online	Keep clients engaged	To make sure our way of working first with our clients' preferences and demands
A greater demand for knowledge	Making sure new opportunities are identified and pursued	To make sure we provide all of the updates and knowledge our clients need in the way they want it
A preference to do things for themselves (for personal and financial reasons)	Managing the return to the office in the way that best suits our lawyers and our clients	To market effectively to our chosen market/s to maximise new opportunities
	Protect the firm and its clients against potential new threats	To adopt and implement the technology that will make the firm more effective and more profitable
		To adapt our current processes to make the firm more client-friendly and more efficient

Figure 8: How to balance preferences, considerations, and objectives.

While you set your objectives it is also important to bear in mind that the tactics required to achieve those objectives will depend on the type of return your particular market ends up seeing. Although none of us knows exactly what that will be, there are three likely outcomes.

A rapid return

A residual demand for services means you'll simply pick up where you left off and your fee levels will return almost as quickly as they fell in the current downturn.

If that is the case you may need to look at:

- Loading your business development plan towards client and contact development;
- Restoring your headcount to previous levels to meet demand;
- Streamlining your service delivery; and
- Shortening payment terms to redress your cash position.

A slow return

If there is a third or even fourth wave of COVID-19, your return could be prolonged for some practice areas while demand increases for others.

If this is the case, you may need to look at:

- Skewing your marketing and business development towards the practice areas in most demand;
- Ensuring your marketing activities can continue virtually;
- Redeploying your resources internally to ensure clients are fully serviced in the busiest areas; and
- Adopting the technology and processes required to ensure your clients remain supported by your prolonged virtual working model.

A volatile return

If the virus continues to return in spikes intermittently over the next 12-24 months, your return could come in fits and starts. If that is the case you may want to look at:

- Introducing more structure around your client development efforts so you are in the best position to leverage any new opportunities as they arise;

- Planning in 30- or 90-day cycles so you can operate with the required flexibility;
- Introducing ideas that can be switched from "physical" to "virtual" and vice versa with little notice;
- Concentrating on projects that can be delivered internally (i.e. implementing new technology, processes, or systems); and
- Reviewing your pricing, billing, and delivery models as this level of uncertainty could make price sensitivity more acute.

How do you choose the right tactics?

In the previous chapter we looked at the internal and external factors that influence the way law firms market, operate, and deliver. This should provide you with enough of an understanding of the way your clients' personal and working lives, behaviors, and attitudes are changing to formulate a strategy that will respond to your new trading environment.

However, even the best strategy will struggle to deliver the success you want if you don't get your tactics right. As every law firm is defined by its people, its specialisms, its location, and its ambitions, it is impossible to say what the right tactics for you would be. Instead, here are five questions you can ask yourselves during your planning process to help you decide.

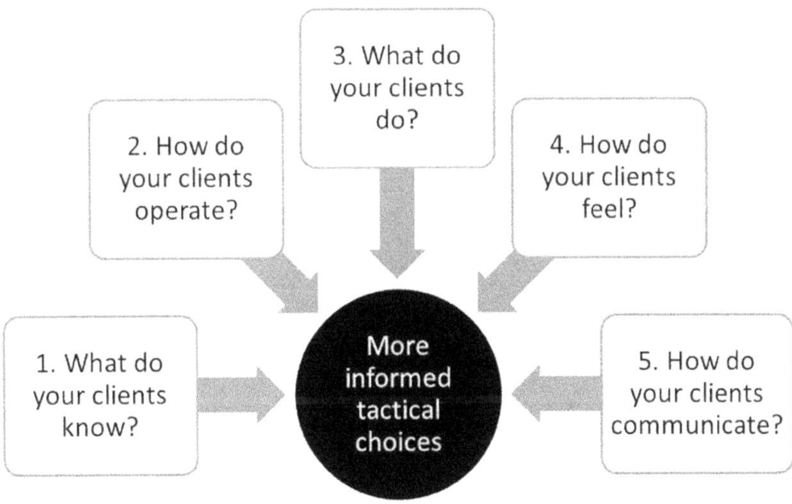

Figure 9: Five questions that will help you make better tactical decisions.

1. What do your clients know?

The answer to this question can be approached from both an internal and external perspective.

The external perspective

This will involve you approaching your clients from two sides.

Firstly, your client development activities and your day-to-day contact with clients will soon unearth the things they don't really understand. It may be that they ask you questions or that when you bring things up you are met with an awkward delayed silence on the other end of the phone or from the other side of the table. This means there is an opportunity to educate your clients.

Secondly, it involves staying up to date with what is going on in your market/s and developing the ability to comment on these things and, where possible, putting that all-important legal spin on the story.

Some of the best examples I have seen of being able to do this have come from a patent attorney and a private client solicitor I work with. The patent attorney immediately jumped on the "Can AI be granted a patent?" bandwagon. As he had a fully formed and very cogent opinion on this (and doesn't mind sharing it!), he managed to broker a series of interviews, editorial and panel positions. This quickly positioned him as a leading expert even though the argument was only just starting to take shape in the UK.

Meanwhile the private client solicitor, bored of writing the same "Why everyone needs a will" article, decided that there was far more to say if she married a personal interest – ethical investment – with her professional area, wealth protection. This provided her with a much more unique platform from which to promote her practice. Again, this quickly led to editorial and speaking opportunities that have really boosted her profile.

The internal perspective

You want to know that your clients know everything about you. More specifically, you want to make sure your business development efforts are continually positioning and repositioning you as the solution, should your clients need additional legal services to those they most regularly purchase.

For example, if a client uses you for commercial contract work, how do you make sure they know about the complete range of contractual work you could do? How could you broker introductions to your colleagues in employment and real estate? How can you ensure you are in pole position should the stakeholders of the business need to rewrite their will or draft a prenuptial agreement?

With regards to tactics, creating awareness of your other services could involve:

- Producing a constant flow of "situationist" content. This means taking situations familiar to your clients and using these to illustrate what else you could be doing for them with real life examples involving advice from your other practice areas;
- Ensuring all of your educational activities have input from all of the relevant practice areas;
- Adopting a more structured approach to introducing colleagues from other disciplines to clients but making those introductions using hooks you've identified either during a matter or as a result of a topic of conversation that arose during your client development activities; and
- Working more closely with key referrers to produce joint marketing ventures that look more broadly at both parties' inherent skillsets.

2. How do your clients operate?

This is a question that will largely be answered while you are talking to your clients (and your professional contacts). However, don't forget just how much latent knowledge you have within the firm already. The various repositories of knowledge that exist in your lawyers' heads should also be tapped into. They will complement the market insight you are collecting via your client development activities.

Before the pandemic you probably had a very good idea as to how your clients operated and what they wanted to do long-term. This could well have changed during COVID-19.

Businesses may have been forced to close branch offices, reduce head-count, or discontinue certain product lines. Conversely, they could have diversified or acquired new additions given there are bargains to be had during any recession. They could have changed their internal processes and/or the way they go to market. They may simply have come to the decision that enough is enough and if they are at that stage of life, it's time to sell.

All of these changes in circumstances may require new types of legal support. Alternatively, if the client's plans are just at the ideas stage, your perspective on how best to proceed could be invaluable in terms of deciding upon their next steps.

If your clients are individuals, they too will have changed the way they go about their lives. The huge changes we have all been through could have prompted them to re-evaluate what they want to do in terms of protecting both their and their families' futures.

It's been widely reported that there was a spike in will writing at the start of the pandemic as people began to feel their own mortality. Unfortunately, divorce rates also rose steeply as a result of couples being locked down together for long periods. All of these changes will require legal assistance.

But there are also more positive aspects. More people are deciding to move house (around the relevant restrictions of course) and the predicted change to the way our cities work moving forward will undoubtedly create demand to move out of cities into quieter satellite towns.

Alternatively, if clients have sold businesses or expedited their retirement plans they may want to update the way they manage and protect their assets both for themselves and their families.

From a tactical perspective, much of your marketing and business development will again come down to how you engage, educate, and update your client base.

However, any suggestions you offer should be provided in a purely practical context. This will demonstrate you are not only a good lawyer but a good lawyer who genuinely understands the nuances of your clients' lives. This approach will make you a much more attractive option than a more generalist competitor. Similarly, digging into the detail of your clients' lives will also position you to take full advantage of third party marketing opportunities.

As with the patent attorney and private client lawyer mentioned in the last section, you will position yourself as an expert. An expert is what your professional contacts want to introduce to their clients. An expert is what conference producers want as speakers and what editors want as authors.

Finally, taking an interest in how your clients operate is also an evergreen reason to catch up with them. Even if you're worried about the amount of potentially billable time those catch-ups can take while all hands are on the pump, consider the value of the insight you'll gain. This insight will inform and drive every other aspect of your business development plan.

3. What do your clients do?

From a purely tactical point of view, once you know what your clients do, you can do it too. And by doing it, you'll be putting yourself in the best possible position of meeting more people just like your clients, which will have an immediate and positive effect on your business development.

Depending on whether your practice has a commercial or a personal focus, you can find out which events your clients go to, which groups they belong to, what they read, and which websites they use.

Tactically this additional layer of insight means:

- If you have chosen to pursue speaking slots, you'll be speaking at the right events;
- If you have chosen to pursue editorial opportunities, you'll be writing in the right publications (i.e. the ones your clients and prospective clients read);
- If you're planning on joining a networking group, you'll find the most relevant ones; and
- If you're joining a trade body, you'll join the most productive one.

Once you know that you can make more informed marketing decisions as to where you spend your time and your budget, cutting out the unknown element ("well this might work") will immediately make your business development become more productive and more time-efficient. It will also make it less of a chore because you will see results.

The other side of knowing what your clients do is you can better tailor your social events and one-on-one meetings. If you know a particular group of clients like food and drink, you can bring them together for a virtual event with a food and drink theme.

Or, if you know that a group like the outdoors, perhaps you could consider setting up a running group or a "walk and talk" or "netwalking" group. This is a new idea that allows you to meet your contacts and clients at an acceptable social distance and is a business development option that is quickly growing in popularity. Again, this is all about using what you know to make more informed – and, by extension, more productive and more profitable – marketing decisions.

4. How do your clients feel?

With so much uncertainty around, any marketing decisions you do make need to be cross-referenced with emotional intelligence. If you get your tone wrong, you could find you alienate a percentage of your audience. While in some markets bullishness is an attractive quality, this is certainly not the case at the moment. People need support, empathy, and reassurance.

Whether you are planning to run educational events online, increase your content production, launch a podcast or write or speak for third parties, make sure everything you do is anchored around solutions.

More importantly, give everything a positive spin. Make sure all of your content is focused on an eventual happy ending and what you need to do to make sure what happens next is a personal and commercial success.

In some markets there may be a groundswell of a certain types of feelings. In areas that have been particularly hard hit by the virus there will be increased anxiety. What can you do from a professional point of view to reduce that anxiety? If you specialize in sectors that have been significantly affected by local restrictions – for example, retail and hospitality – can you build a "road back" type campaign that will guide your clients back to where they were?

The other point to consider is how clients feel about you. Community has been a huge consideration for the majority of us during the past few months. Many firms have reconnected with their local or business communities through volunteering, pro bono work, and donations. If you feel you may still be more distant from the communities your clients are involved in, this may be a time to re-evaluate the different strands of your plan to see if you could make tactical decisions that would reduce that distance.

5. How do your clients communicate?

This is probably the most straightforward factor. Depending on the age, tech-friendliness, and profile of your clients you can make assumptions as to the best ways of getting your message across to your market/s. As we discussed earlier in the book, if you are providing private client and wealth protection services to an older client base you would probably not use the same channels as you would for tech start-ups.

Data is again important when it comes to finalizing your decisions. In the past (and if you can compare the recent past to your pre-COVID-19 past you will obtain even more valuable results), what methods of communication worked best? Did you get more engagement from social media or Google? Does your audience react better to video or words? With video, was it your pieces to camera or your infographics that worked best? With words, did people react better to a newsletter that included advice from a range of practice areas or a bullet point "listicle" telling them what to do in a certain situation?

On a more personal level, make a note of which client prefers which method of communication and pander to those preferences. Some may like a letter but others may like texts or WhatsApp messages. Others may prefer a good old fashioned phone call. Using all the other functions on your smartphone is not selling out your profession; it is providing the service your clients want. This will strengthen the personal side of your working relationships.

What can you do today?

It's been said repeatedly throughout this book, but we are in a state of flux at the moment. However, uncertainty is not an excuse for inaction. Returning your firm to where it was will require you to invest the time and effort to build your plan and put it into action.

As things will remain uncertain for some time to come, it is highly likely that your plan will need to be tweaked as circumstances and demand becomes clearer, but as long as you set objectives you are comfortable with and the tactics you have chosen have been informed by your clients and your understanding of the market, it will hold up.

Don't get waylaid by the pursuit of perfection. Perfection isn't achievable, especially as there are so many things we don't know for sure yet. Instead, commit to your plan and always remember the wise words of General George S Patton:

> *"A good plan well executed now is always better than a perfect plan executed next week."*

In terms of setting your first actions, the following tips may help you get your implementation underway.

Create an implementation team

While your return will involve everyone in the firm in some capacity, progress will be more likely if it's driven by a few well-chosen members of staff from each department. The members of your implementation do not all need to be fee earners. You may want to include the senior members of your marketing, finance, HR, and IT teams as they will all have a more informed view of their particular pillars.

Retain your best people

I can't sugar-coat this; morale across the firm has probably dipped over the last few months. Furlough, redundancy, and an uncertain future will have combined with the feelings of isolation caused by working from home. This needs to be addressed directly. Tell your people they are valued, reassure them that they have a specific part to play in your return, and if you have made changes to your remuneration or incentives, this is the time to tell them.

Get everyone onboard

Silence now will be damaging later. If people don't know what's expected of them (and why), they won't be able to play their part. Once you have your plan, share it as soon as possible. This cannot be done by email. Bring everyone together for a detailed and interactive session and invite questions and even challenges so everyone understands every part of the plan and why you have chosen to take this direction.

Once you have launched your plan, make sure you keep your staff updated on progress. Even when a launch is met positively, the memory can soon fade away if it's allowed to. Your plan needs to be a living, breathing thing. It can't be received and forgotten as "the latest idea from management".

Don't talk about crisis, talk about return

The implementation of your plan is going to be hard enough with so much uncertainty around, so make sure you're using the right language. Give your launch and all your subsequent updates a positive spin.

You are not fighting fires, papering over cracks, or holding things together with a band aid. You are taking very deliberate steps to return the firm where it was pre-pandemic.

You are returning your fee levels, your client base, and your profit levels to where they were whilst implementing a new way of working that reflects the best of what we've learned since March with the best of what you've always done.

You are refreshing the firm so that it better meets the new demands of your clients, which will return the firm's relationships to their former glory and, by extension, return the firm to being a safe and secure place of work.

Review and refresh

Even with the best will in the world you won't get your plan totally right first time around. Don't worry. The law of "adapt, improvise, and overcome" will always come to your rescue.

However, you do need to stay attuned to what needs to be adapted, improvised, and overcome. Your management committee and/or implementation team needs to continually review your progress. They also need to reflect on what you've learned and what you're seeing other organizations doing.

Partly this is because the more you know, the more improvements you'll be able to make, but it's also to make sure you're not caught short by the likely continuing changes in your own circumstances and in your market/s in general.

Chapter 12: And finally...

When it comes to launching your new plan there are two fundamental critical success factors you will need to actively manage – implementation and motivation. I thought it might be useful to end by sharing some best practice that will help you deal with both more effectively.

Successful implementation

Once you have your plan and you are ready to move from launch to implementation, these four steps will maximize your likelihood of success:

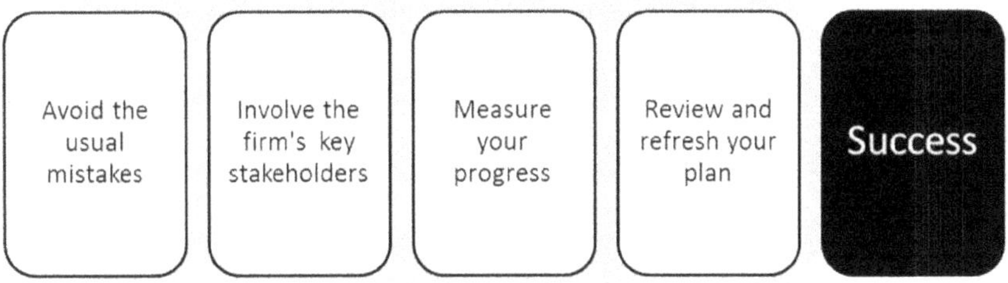

Figure 10: The successful implementation model.

Avoid the usual mistakes

It doesn't matter how strong your plan is, there are always a number of things that can go wrong when it moves off the page and into real life. However, forewarned is forearmed so here are a few factors you should be mindful of.

"Personal pockets" form

Certain pockets within the firm may try to discard the plan, choosing instead to pursue a different course in isolation for their personal benefit. This cannot be allowed to happen. If even only a few people start to do their own thing your plan will crack, progress will falter, and everyone involved will end up confused as to what they should be doing. Confusion never leads to success.

Communication stops

Despite an initial flurry of communications during the launch, that level of communication can dip once people get back to their desks to be confronted by the usual client and billing pressures.

Keep communicating (particularly your successes), keep your staff focused on your goals, and keep asking for feedback from those on the front line.

Avoid the onset of "bolt-on" syndrome

Make sure that your plan is viewed as an enabler, a route map that needs to be followed. If it starts to be viewed as something that is either separate to the "day job" or something that only the senior partners need to be concerned with, you will lose momentum.

Your plan is now "business as usual"

Again, your plan is a route map so it has to become the embodiment of "business as usual". You cannot afford for heads of department or pockets of the firm to nod and agree during the launch only to go back to what they've always done at the first opportunity.

Avoid avoidance

Sometimes people can try to avoid taking the action required to support the tougher choices you've made in your plan. For your plan to succeed you need to make sure it's followed even though some actions may cause some short-term discomfort.

Mis-measurement

Make sure those who are tasked with measuring progress are reporting everything they should be and reporting accurately. You need to be able to see the full picture, not just the parts that will show certain people in the best light.

Maintain a 360 purview

If you are only measuring what's happening inside the firm you may miss vital macro indicators. Try to monitor what is happening around you, particularly with regards to your competitors. This does not mean instigating an unhealthy obsession with your competitors and trying to copy everything they're doing (which would doubtless be at odds with your plan); it means ensuring you are staying in line with client, market, and price expectations.

KISS

As the saying goes, Keep It Simple, Stupid. Keep your plan simple so that everyone understands it. Sometimes as things are added or adapted, all sorts of jargon and management speak can creep in. This not only confuses people, it can put them off participating entirely.

Involve the firm's key stakeholders

Once your plan is up and running you will need to communicate progress regularly to all of the firm's employees and keep reminding them what their personal responsibilities within the delivery are.

Within your communications encourage your staff to share their experiences and suggest new ideas or ways to improve the delivery. In many cases those on the frontline can add enormous value because they are so close to both their clients and their markets.

To maximize the level of involvement in your plan it may be worth including strategic updates in all of your departmental meetings. You could also add it as a discussion point to your appraisal structure in case some employees are more comfortable putting their point of view away from the eyes and ears of their colleagues. Or, if you want to allow complete anonymity, you could put suggestion boxes in communal areas.

Also, remember your stakeholders are not just inside the firm. Your clients and your professional and industry contacts are also stakeholders, so make sure they are involved too.

Share your strategic plan with them and ask them what they think and where they feel your plan could be improved. Not only will this inject a flattering level of inclusivity, it also provides a perfect opportunity for you to spend time with your most important external stakeholders and, as we've discussed, these conversations very rarely pass without creating new fee opportunities.

Measure your progress

The only way to find out how well the implementation of your plan is going is to measure and record the key indicators. While some of these will be financial indicators (gross fee revenue and profitability), the majority will be performance indicators. For example:

- How many client visits have you made?
- How many new pieces of content have you published?
- How many events have you run?
- How many presentations have you given?
- How many external editorial slots have you won?
- How much press coverage has the firm received?

In the early stages of your implementation these are the results that matter most. This is the type of activity that boosts your profile and starts conversations and the financial results will follow when you get that part right.

Although it's slightly less tangible, you may also want to measure client satisfaction. You will be introducing new ideas and trying new things so it is worth asking your clients what they think of your new ways of working and communicating. You also need to provide them with an easy way to make their own suggestions as to what else you could do to improve your offering and delivery.

One possible way of gathering that feedback would be to ask your clients for a testimonial. This would allow them to summarize their experience of working with the firm. You can use these statements to refresh and add a much more personal dimension to your marketing materials.

However, while you are in conversation you can also naturally start to probe a little deeper, which could well lead to new fee opportunities.

Review and refresh your plan

If your plan is going to be a living and breathing thing rather than just another piece of paper, you will need to continually review it and, where necessary, refresh certain parts.

Measuring your progress properly requires you to monitor all of your key performance indicators consistently. If you do that, you will be able to see which parts are working and which aren't. These figures can be provided on a personal, departmental, and firm level and reviewed by either your management or BD committee or by your implementation team.

With regards to the practical side of setting up an effective review and refresh structure, these tips may help.

Set your milestones (and hit them)

Monitoring your progress will be much easier if you set yourself milestones. Where do you want to be at the end of each quarter? What specifically do you need to achieve during each quarter?

Once you know exactly what needs to be achieved and by when, you have a simple set of milestones that will drive your progress. Your milestones need to be precise. "Increase profile" is too woolly. Your milestones should be based on hard numbers.

Set your timetable (and stick to it)

You probably need to review your progress on a quarterly basis – any less frequently and things can slip and any more frequently and you may not have anything worthwhile to report. This shouldn't be an overly long or arduous task. If you are reporting through the ranks it should be easy to collate an accurate snapshot of what has been achieved over the previous quarter.

The best way to explain reporting through the ranks is to borrow from a scene in The Godfather Pt II. During the committee hearings into the mafia, a witness produces a graphic that shows how the soldiers kick up to the captains and the captains then kick up to the boss. Your firm should work in a similar way. Your lawyers' personal efforts will feed into your departments' efforts, which will then feed into the firm's plan.

The one thing that halts progress more often than anything else is a shortage of time. Some lawyers will say they didn't have time to collect their figures or even that they don't have time to attend the review meeting itself. Don't accept this; being too busy is not an acceptable reason for non-adherence. This is everyone's firm so delivering the plan is everyone's responsibility.

If there are justifiable reasons that progress hasn't been made – i.e. the required support, resource, tech, or budget hasn't been forthcoming – these reasons should be remedied during your review. If they're left unchecked they will continue to hamper your progress.

Don't be afraid to challenge

While you're measuring your plan's progress, continue to discuss the validity of overarching objectives, particularly in the context of the most recent changes within your market. If there are another series of wholesale changes to the way people live and work because of prolonged and repeated spikes in the virus or because self-preservation demands we work in yet another new way, you will need to react to those to ensure your offering and advice remain relevant to your market/s.

Don't be polite or overly reverent to your initial plan. Use your meetings to table concerns and observations and challenge the validity of the parts of your plan you think may need to be refreshed.

Continue to upskill

If actions are not being completed because the lawyers responsible for their delivery don't have the requisite skills, you will need to provide training on those areas.

This goes for your support teams too. If, for example, your plan involves you increasing your share of the charities market and success will require you to increase your tender conversion rates, you need to provide your marketers with tender training or access to an external expert who can work with them to improve your in-house capabilities.

Training is crucial to the success of new technology too. You will never see the true value from new systems if people don't know how to use them properly. If the skills gaps are more extreme or the next phase of your plan requires you to increase capability in a particular area of the law, you may need to recruit. As the recruitment process tends to take six months or longer, depending on the seniority of the people you need, you need to start the ball rolling on lateral hires as early as possible.

Reward success

Law firms are often good at critiquing their lawyers' performance, but not as good at celebrating successes. Find ways to communicate your successes to everyone in the firm. Pick people out for particular praise when they have brought in a significant new client or been involved in a particularly well-received BD activity. Report when you've hit significant milestones in your plan. If you can, introduce financial rewards for those who continually deliver. If these people are out-performing their targets, a percentage of that additional revenue can be re-appropriated so the firm is not incurring any additional cost.

Successful motivation

However strong your plan is and however well you manage its implementation, it won't be able to generate the results it should if your colleagues are not suitably motivated to play their part.

While it's never been possible to keep all of your people fully motivated all of the time, the current situation has made the task even harder. With people working on their own from different locations, the worry of catching the virus, and the possible consequences of the ongoing economic uncertainty, levels of morale and motivation have understandably dipped.

As your people have such a vital role to play in making sure your firm enjoys a successful future, here are a few tips to help keep them loyal, productive, and motivated even while they are working as virtual lawyers.

Stay positive

While we are communicating virtually it is easy for emails and other written communications to be misinterpreted. Similarly, overly officious language or brevity (for example, not adding a note to a forwarded email or, worse, putting your instructions in the subject line and leaving the email blank) can cause irritation.

Remember, it's not what you say but how you say it. Although you too will be under more stress than usual, try to adopt a conversational and informal tone. Don't forget to ask people about life outside work and be prepared to make a bit of small talk.

Most importantly, stay positive. Endless missives on the doom and gloom that the COVID-19 situation has inflicted on the firm will inevitably (and subliminally) prompt people to react negatively. Instead, provide a positive outlook (even if that requires selective editing of the facts) and keep your focus on the brighter future and how you're going to get there.

Keep communicating

Just as communication is central to the successful implementation of your plan, it is also a motivational prerequisite. Maintaining an "open door policy" (even if the open door is actually a window on your staff's screens) is vital. Explain what you are doing and why and encourage them to offer feedback and put forward ideas that will help deliver your vision.

If there is bad news on the horizon, make sure you pre-empt the office gossips by providing a full explanation (with as much positive spin as you can give it) so you restrict the damage to morale an ill-informed version could inflict.

Create inclusivity

Transparency and communication are important but they are not enough. You should not only court feedback but be seen to be using that feedback. People need to feel included and that means taking every opportunity to show them they are playing an active role in shaping the next chapter of the firm.

Recognize achievement

Successes need to be reported. Publicly recognizing the good things your team are achieving and praising them – by name – for their accomplishments will help you show your colleagues you appreciate them. However, sometimes it is the smallest things that have the biggest impact.

Bonuses and commissions are nice but as the financial position of most firms is still a little precarious, a financial reward may not always be possible. If that is the case, could you send them flowers, wine, or chocolates? Could you provide tickets to a virtual comedy night or concert? Could you simply give them an early start to the weekend?

Don't publicize failure

The flipside of recognizing achievement is not publicizing failure. Calling people out publicly in front of their colleagues is a sure fire way to damage motivation. Accept that we all make mistakes; it's just part of being human. It's also more likely to happen while we're working remotely.

If a mistake has been made, take time out to see how and why it occurred. Then, in private, reassure your colleague that this is a learning opportunity, not a punishable offence, and work out what training or changes are needed to make sure it doesn't happen again.

Control work/life balance

At the start of the pandemic a lot of firms furloughed a portion of their staff. This left a smaller team with more work to do. As the pressure of dividing the work between fewer lawyers started to mount, motivation dropped like a stone.

There are, of course, financial and economic realities to face, but if you are going to keep your team onside you need to do what you can to control their work/life balance. There will be times when client demands will extend the working day – but could you give your team some of that time back during quieter periods? Even this small gesture will show you have their best interests at heart.

The last thing you want at the moment is key people leaving because their practice has taken over their lives. Aside from leaving you temporarily shorthanded, which could impact on the consistency of service your clients receive, finding and integrating their replacements could be a long and expensive process. These are costs you would probably prefer not to have to cover at the moment.

Aside from the personal aspects of overwork, there are also more professional reasons for controlling your lawyers' work/life balance. If people are working too much for a prolonged period of time the quality of their work will drop and crucial details could be missed. This will irritate your clients and, as we've discussed throughout this book, you cannot afford for your clients to be unsettled while you are working so hard to return your firm to its former position.

Sustain progression and development

As things are much less clear at the moment, the fear that traditional opportunities to progress and develop may have been put on hold could be playing on your lawyers' minds. Left unchecked, these feelings can grow into dissatisfaction, which will over time affect motivation levels.

Make sure you are continuing to offer professional and "soft skills" training. This will show you are still committed to developing your people. You can also set clear goals for the people who have demonstrated an ambition to progress up the ladder so they feel they are actively working towards realizing those ambitions.

Keep a routine

Whether you are working at home, in the office, or somewhere in between, make sure you are keeping a routine. Routine means normality and we all need to grab all the normality we can at the moment. Keep to your regular team meeting structure, provide reports at the same rate as you would usually, and ensure you are having your regular one-on-ones (even if they are being held virtually).

If at all possible you can also try to set boundaries to the working day and dissuade people from working at weekends. As a lot of us have desks in our living rooms and spare bedrooms at the moment, so it's very easy to fall into keeping longer and more disjointed hours. This is not a routine!

The only issue here is some lawyers actually like the fact they can set their own hours so putting too much routine in might cause the opposite effect and actually demotivate them. So that you get it right, talk to your colleagues so you know what works best for them.

Pay your people properly

Many lawyers have taken either furlough or a cut in pay or hours during the pandemic. Neither of these things will improve motivation. If you have had to take these steps, make sure you communicate when normal service will return and try to find performance-based incentives to bridge at least some of the gap.

When things are more normal you should also complete a review of the pay and conditions your competitors are offering. The last thing you want is for key members of staff to leave for an incremental pay rise after you worked so hard to keep them employed during the crisis and have put so much effort into creating a firm capable of providing them with long-term stability.

Find reasons for collaboration

A little more personal contact (even if it's via video) is a simple way to boost morale. From an internal perspective, find reasons to get lawyers talking to other lawyers across the firm, whether it's because they are working on shared clients or shared cross-departmental projects. From an external perspective, encourage business development activities that involve collaborating with clients and professional and industry contacts.

Just as collaborative marketing initiatives give us a reason to talk to our contacts, partial secondments to clients or discussions on how to increase service levels could provide the same opportunities to collaborate with clients.

Don't micromanage

It is unbelievably demotivating to feel there's always someone looking over your shoulder while you're working. If you have set out your team's goals, they will know what they need to do. You should be able to let them get on with it, catching up as usual (sticking to your routine) to discuss progress and support requirements.

If you don't have your own line management responsibilities and feel you are being micromanaged to the detriment of your own motivation levels, tell your manager you need a little more space while you continue to complete the actions and tasks you've been set.

Avoid unnecessary (and unnecessarily long) meetings

While some meetings are needed, many aren't. It's estimated the average professional spends almost four hours per week in unnecessary meetings. You need to identify these and cut them out.

You can also make the meetings you do need to have shorter and more productive with minimal effort. Set and distribute an agenda ahead of the meeting so people can prepare and provide their updates succinctly.

When meetings are necessary you should also be respectful of your colleagues' time by starting and ending on time. There is nothing more demotivating than sitting waiting for the last person to arrive because they obviously feel their time is more valuable than the combined time being wasted by everyone waiting for them.

Offer greater flexibility

While we don't know exactly when we will be able to make a full return to the office, the time we've had to spend working from home seems to have divided lawyers into two distinct camps – those who can't wait to get back to the office and those who want to continue working from home.

However and whenever our offices open fully, you will need to offer your people a choice as to how they want to work. Even the most traditional firms who probably want a full return have to accept that their competitors will be offering greater flexibility. This means they could become more attractive employers if some members of your staff have been demotivated by being told where and when to work.

Another strong argument for greater flexibility is that many firms actually reported a rise in productivity while their lawyers were working remotely. It showed that the lingering specter of presentism was – as we all knew – outmoded and ineffective. It is results that count, not hours on-site.

However, while all of these tips will work within the legal environment, when it comes to successfully maintaining motivation there is one other quick and relatively inexpensive option – team building.

Ensuring your team members keep a personal, if virtual, connection is crucial to keeping them motivated. As part of a team there is more inclination to participate in the required actions. It will also open more lines of communication, which will add some much needed variety to the working day.

We have already looked at the potential value of running virtual hospitality events for clients and contacts but it is equally important to ruin similar events for our teams, particularly around the times of year the firm has traditionally run its staff events.

With the way things are it may be some time before the whole firm can get together for its annual conference or a full-scale party. Even lunches and dinners are difficult depending on the trading restrictions being placed on the hospitality sector and the need to remain socially distant. It is also difficult to organize any events involving sports or creative activities for the same reasons.

Drinks and evening socials over Zoom have become rather tired and anecdotal evidence suggests attendance (and, more importantly, enthusiasm) is dropping in most firms. However, all of the same virtual options we looked at under client development are still possibilities. The increased availability of online cookery lessons, cocktail making sessions, escape rooms, and comedy evenings means that there are a number of options you could consider.

While team building may just sound like one more thing to organize and pay for, it will pay you back. It underlines how much you appreciate your colleagues and shows you are prepared to really invest in keeping your team together at a time when we are largely being forced to work apart as virtual lawyers.

www.ingramcontent.com/pod-product-compliance
Ingram Content Group UK Ltd.
Pitfield, Milton Keynes, MK11 3LW, UK
UKHW021849150926
8657IPUK00005B/154

9 781783 584024